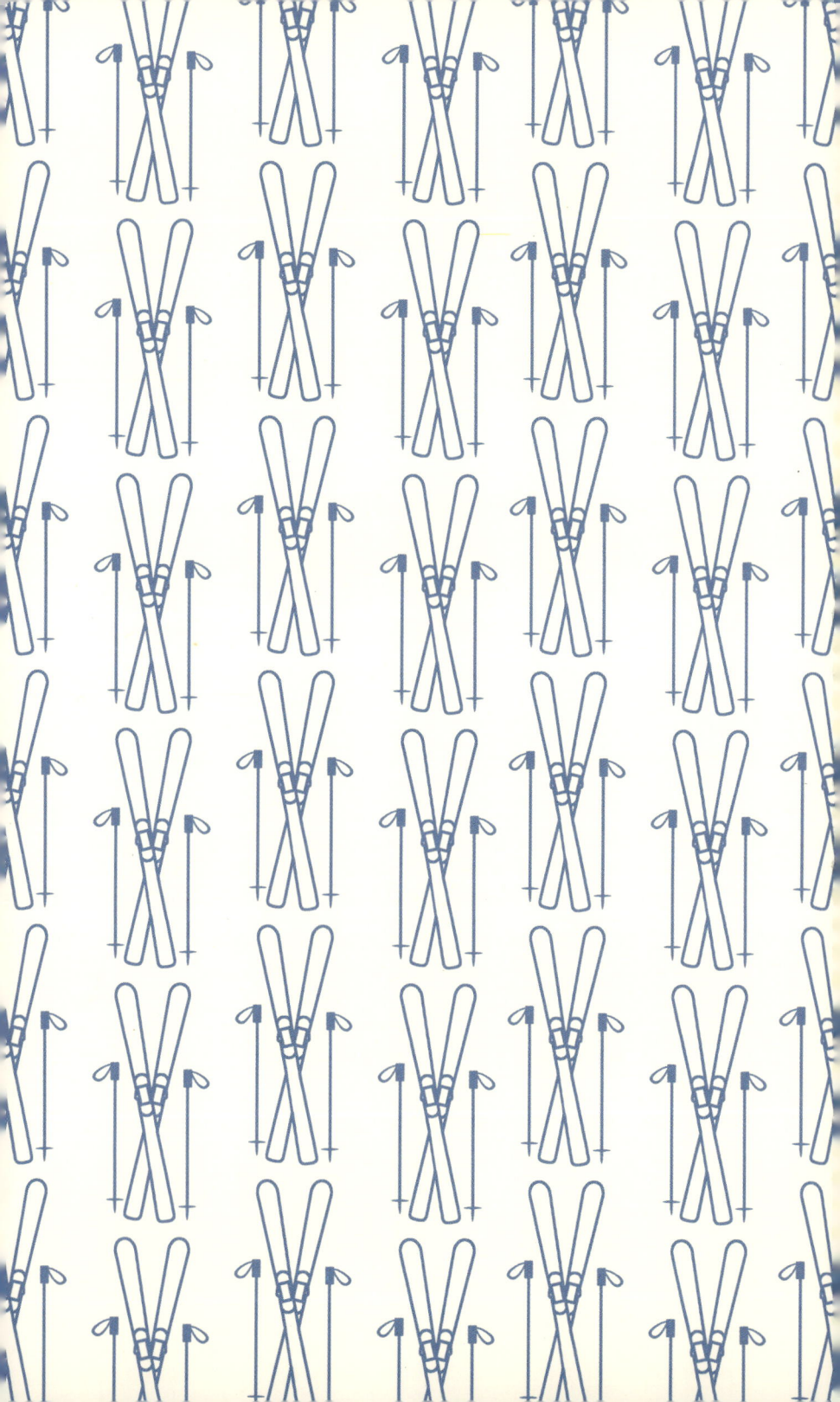

HIKE THE COURSE

A JOURNEY OF FAMILY,
PASSION AND OLYMPIC SUCCESS
FOR INSPIRING AND TRANSFORMING
ATHLETES OF ALL AGES

BARBARA ANN COCHRAN

Hike the Course: A Journey of Family, Passion and Olympic Success for Inspiring and Transforming Athletes of all Ages

Copyright © 2023 by Barbara Ann Cochran

All rights reserved. No part of this publication may be reproduced, distributed, or transmitted in any form or by any means, including photocopying, recording or other electronic or mechanical methods, without the prior written permission of the author, except in the case of brief quotations embodied in reviews and certain other non-commercial uses permitted by copyright law.

Without in any way limiting the author's [and publisher's] exclusive rights under copyright, any use of this publication to "train" generative artificial intelligence (AI) technologies to generate text is expressly prohibited. The author reserves all rights to license uses of this work for generative AI training and development of machine learning language models.

Printed in the United States of America
Hardcover ISBN: 978-1-960876-50-8
Paperback ISBN: 978-1-960876-51-5
Ebook ISBN: 978-1-960876-52-2
Library of Congress Control Number: 2023920383

Muse Literary
3319 N. Cicero Avenue
Chicago IL 60641-9998

This book is dedicated to my Dad,
who started it all with his dream
to build a rope-tow in the backyard.

Prologue

**My Olympic Story
1972 Sapporo, Japan**

At the Winter Olympics in 1972, I was right there with all the new stars in ski racing—Annemarie Proell, Michele Jacot, Marie-Therese Nadig, and my sister, Marilyn Cochran. Then there were the names that we already knew—Wiltrud Drexel, Annie Famose, and Isabelle Mir. For some, the Games would be a beginning; for others, this would be the end.

My last race was the slalom. As I walked up the hill to inspect the course, cold, wet flakes fell all around me. I went slowly, step by step and gate by gate, taking the time to memorize the turns, the bumps, and the terrain. For the majority of the course, everything was smooth and rhythmical. The only tough spots were the bumps.

I skied a couple of runs and felt good. All I had left to do was wait for the start. I ran number 1. I felt good about that, too.

Ten minutes before the race, the rep checked my bindings and the coach spread wax on my skis. I pumped my legs up and down to get the blood flowing, feeling my heartbeat increase with the anticipation.

Seven minutes left. I unzipped my warm-ups and handed them to my coach. The wind whipped snow into my face and chilled my muscles. I slid into the tent.

Four minutes. The first forerunner stepped into the starting gate. The coach rubbed my legs to increase my circulation. I took a deep breath, trying to relax.

Three! The forerunner left. Another moved into place.

Two! I pulled off my parka and was left alone.

One! I stepped up to the gate. There were twenty seconds left to wait. I planted my poles.

Ten seconds! I took three deep breaths. Five, four, three, two, one, GO!

I lunged out of the start, feeling the cold wind on my face. The first turns were impossibly slow. I swung through the open gates, up under the hairpin, and across the hill. Then I was flying over the bumps.

Good! I was through. The flags blurred, but I only reacted, seeing the finish line up ahead. Three last quick turns and then I was skating and straining to get through. I stopped, looked at my time, and waited.

Britt Lafforgue was number 3. She had won the last slalom. If my time held up against hers, I should do well. She finished just two-tenths behind me. I had a chance!

Then I waited for Daniele Debernard. She was young and would go all out. She looked good. When her time lit up on the board, I felt elated. I was ahead of her by three-hundredths!

My sister, Marilyn, started and fell. I watched a few more ski racers and my excitement grew. I was leading after the first run! I had a chance to win!

But I knew I had to calm down. I had another course to memorize and one more run to complete. I tried to focus and learn the course, but I couldn't concentrate. When my coach skied down to me and handed me my parka and warm-ups, he had a smile on his face, but he didn't say much.

Then Marilyn stopped to pick up her parka, her silence showing how disappointed she was in her run. She talked to the coach for a minute and then burst into tears. The slalom was her last race, too. I knew how much she wanted to do well in the

PROLOGUE

Olympics and felt bad for her.

My sister looked up and managed a smile for me. She was happy that I was ahead and wished me luck for the next run.

I continued on my way, fighting to stay calm. My thoughts wandered in all different directions, focusing on all of the wrong things, and I started to choke.

It all started when I thought, *I really could win an Olympic gold medal!* Then many questions ran through my head: *Could I do it? Could I put down a good second run? What did I have to do to keep the lead?*

My mind kept spinning. *I'm in the Olympics—the ultimate race of all time! The pinnacle of what I've been training for—for years! This is it! I want to win! I want to beat those French girls! What if I win an Olympic gold medal?! But what if I don't? What if I fall like Marilyn? What if I mess up? What if I don't ski well?*

The more I let these thoughts take over my mind, the more I could feel myself losing it. I was choking! I was getting too tense! I knew that I wouldn't ski well if I kept this up.

So, I took over my inner voice and started giving myself a little pep talk. I told myself, *Come on, B.A.! You've got to change how you're thinking because, right now, this isn't working!*

I reminded myself, *I can only do my best and that's all that matters.* I continued to build up my confidence, realizing, *If the French girls can win, I can win, too!* But at the same time, I stayed realistic and prepared myself for possible defeat, thinking, *Even if I don't win, I've won the first run and not very many people have done that! I can always be proud of that accomplishment!*

Then I thought of my father who was back at home in Vermont. Two years prior, when we were at the World Championships in Val Gardena, Italy, he told me before my race, "I always thought you were 'the cool cucumber' in the family." I smiled when I remembered that and, finally, I was calm.

I hiked up the rest of the course, zoned back into my

3

surroundings. I was confident that I could learn it now and was happy to realize that it wasn't difficult at all. In fact, this course was much straighter and a little faster than the first one; I knew that I would do all right.

The minutes passed and the second run was starting. This time, I ran fifteenth.

The fog moved in, and the visibility dropped. The wind blew and the snow still fell. I could only see five gates out of the start.

Daniele left, followed by Britt. I didn't know how they did. Honestly, I didn't care. I just wanted to focus on doing my best.

I moved up to the gate and waited for the countdown. I was the cool cucumber of the Cochrans. I knew that I had this.

Behind me, I heard Marilyn shout, "Good luck!"

Then, I was on the course!

The gates slid past me. My mind was numb. Turn after turn, I had no thoughts except to get to the finish. I kept going, my mind steeled and determined, and then I was through.

I had made it! I knew that I could have won, but I was too scared to look up at the scoreboard and find out. Looking around, I was stunned to hear only silence.

Then I heard my boyfriend and my brother yell in excitement. I looked up to see Rick and Bob tumbling over the fence and run over to me. I was immediately showered with hugs and kisses, and they hoisted me up on their shoulders.

Then, I knew. I had won!

As I soon found out, I had won by the closest margin in history up to that point. Daniele Debernard, who had finished three-hundredths of a second behind me on the first run, beat me by a hundredth in the second run. But, overall, I beat her—by two-hundredths!

I was so glad that I didn't find out that she had beat everyone else by nearly a whole second in that last run until I was finished.

I'm not sure I would have been able to hold onto my confidence. I would have doubted my ability and started thinking all of those crazy questions again. At that point, I would have stopped believing in myself and started trying too hard.

The important thing was that I didn't have a clue how anyone else had done. I just did my very best and accepted that all I could ask of myself was to put my best effort into the run. That's all it took! Once I put my best effort into it, that was enough.

The lesson I learned that day? Doing your best is all that counts, and that is good enough!

Part One

CHAPTER 1

The Dream

My Parents

My story about winning the Olympic gold started many years ago—before me—with a dream that my father had to build a rope-tow on a hill behind our farmhouse in the countryside. As my brother and sisters and I grew up and excelled in skiing, the press began to call us "The Skiing Cochrans," and we were publicly known as "America's First Family of Skiing." In many ways, we became famous simply by circumstance, but I also credit a lot of our success to Dad being ahead of his time.

My father—Gordon, or "Mickey," as everyone called him—was born in 1923 to Joseph Sullivan and Grace Eadie in Manchester, New Hampshire. According to family lore, Grandpa Sullivan had a son named Neil from his first marriage, and shortly after the baby's birth, his young wife passed away. Once I found that out, I had reason to believe that Grandpa Sullivan needed a new wife to be the mother to his baby and began looking around until he met Grandma Grace and married her.

At that point in our family history, some tension arose because the Sullivans were Irish Catholics and refused to recognize Grandpa's marriage to Grammy because she was Scottish Protestant. In fact, the Catholic Church actually went so far as to excommunicate Grandpa and ban him from using the family burial plot in the Catholic Cemetery.

Despite all that, the new couple settled down with little Neil, and my dad was born shortly afterwards. When Dad was only one year old, in 1924, Grandpa Sullivan's health began failing due to his exposure to mustard gas during his time serving in World War I. Based on what I found out about the repercussions of being exposed to mustard gas, I believe that Grandpa suffered from anemia, which explained why the hospital performed a blood transfusion from my grandma to my grandpa during that time. Unfortunately, the medical procedure did not work, and Grandpa passed away shortly afterwards.

At that point, Grammy intended to raise both young boys (Neil and Dad), but the Sullivan family took Neil away from her because they still refused to recognize Grammy and Grandpa's marriage. Grammy raised Dad for many years as a single mom.

When Dad was in his early teens, Grammy was working for one of her colleagues as a hairdresser. At one point, the colleague introduced her to her brother, Thomas Cochran, who had immigrated to the U.S. from Scotland when he was only 17 and worked in the shipyards as a ship-builder. As they say, the rest is history!

After Grammy and Grandpa Cochran got married, they had a son, my Uncle Tommy. Growing up, my brother and sisters and I loved Grandpa Cochran because he was the grandfather that we all knew. One of the special things about him that we all thought was so much fun was his authentic Scottish brogue.

On the other side of the family, we actually did not know much about the Sullivans except that they did not accept Dad as one of their own. However, we did meet one of our aunts, who was a nun in the Catholic Church.

I remember when I was around five years old Dad somehow got in touch with Sister Cornelia to see if she could come to visit because she lived in a convent in Claremont, New Hampshire, which was not very far from where we lived in Cornish.

THE DREAM

When the arrangements were made, my dad was so excited! He told all of us the good news. I remember thinking, as a five-year-old, that this was something really special. Dad set up lawn chairs in the yard and Mom prepared some drinks and snacks for them. After Sister Cornelia arrived, the adults sat and visited in the lawn chairs while we kids played. I remember that they enjoyed their time of sharing family stories for quite a while. I remember that Sister Cornelia came to see us another time after that as well.

All throughout his years in school, Dad was an incredible sports player and an excellent student. He participated in baseball, basketball, hockey, football, swimming, and, of course, skiing. Even at a young age, he had an inquisitive mind. He told me about a time, when he was five years old, he had a hard time believing that reindeer could really fly, so he climbed up on a roof and jumped off. He wanted to see if he could fly! When Dad fell to the ground, he figured out that since he couldn't fly, he didn't believe that Santa's reindeer could fly either.

Dad grew up to be an extraordinary young man who was very talented, skilled, and knowledgeable in everything that he did, even carrying all of his abilities into his experience serving in World War II.

Dad rarely told us anything about his war days when we were young. In fact, the only thing that I remember him mentioning was that he had dealt with enough killing in the war to ever make him want to hunt, fish, or do anything like that. Later on, when I was an adult, Dad opened up and shared more with me about what it was like to serve in World War II.

For example, Dad told me how one of his main jobs was to clear the minefields. Because he was very athletic and he thought outside the box, he realized that going into the minefield to disarm the mines was dangerous and likely would get him killed. Instead of going out into the minefield, my dad knew that the right way to diffuse the mines was to examine the ground and recognize any places that looked like small disturbances in the natural terrain because that is where the mines had been planted. At that point, Dad would shoot at the places where the ground seemed to be a little off until all the mines exploded.

Dad also told me about when his unit was patrolling a nearby town and came upon a street that split in two. Dad and one of his buddies were told to check each of the streets for snipers. So, Dad went left, and his buddy went right, and only Dad made it back because his buddy was taken out by a sniper. In that situation, it was more like luck of the draw instead of skill.

Another time, Dad explained what happened after his first battle in Germany. He saw a wagon that was filled with casualties. He recognized two of the dead bodies on top—they were two of his buddies!

In that moment, Dad realized that the likelihood of him making it out of Germany alive was very slim and he thought to himself, *I'm not going home!* But what he shared next was thought-provoking. What he said was, "But you know what? World War II got a lot easier when I knew this was where I was going to die."

At first, I was very surprised to hear that and wondered, *What did he mean?* I finally figured out what he meant, and it made a lot of sense—without thinking about what he had to do to survive, he could focus on his job. There's a lot more freedom in that. He didn't have to waste energy or worry about any decisions other than what he was assigned to do.

As I thought about that over the years and studied athletic performance, I came to a deeper understanding. Essentially, when athletes are trying to avoid making a mistake, we come at it from a negative emphasis. However, when we are free of the undesirable focus, then we have the ability to concentrate on the skills that we are trying to execute instead.

THE DREAM

As for my mom, she was given the name Virginia when she was born, but when she grew up, she was always called by the nickname Gingy. Once she went to college, she decided that she did not like Gingy, so she essentially changed her name to Ginny.

Growing up, Mom was the fourth out of five kids and lived on various farms around Hartland in Vermont. She liked to tell me and my brother and sisters a lot of stories about her childhood, For example, one day, when we were walking through a field, she pointed out a juniper bush to us and began to tell us how she and some of her friends liked to grab a blanket and sleep on top of juniper bushes when it was a nice summer night and watch the stars. At the beginning of the night, it would be a comfortable mattress, but by the morning, the juniper branches would begin to poke through the blankets and become quite unbearable!

Another time, my mom told the story about how she nearly drowned one winter. She and her younger sister, Aunt Harriet, were skating on a pond when the ice cracked, and they both fell through. My mom was able to push Aunt Harriet out of the hole, but she wasn't able to pull herself out, so the two girls cried out for help. Fortunately, there were two boys who were in the woods hunting that heard them shouting, so they ran over and extended a long pole out to Mom so she could grab on and pull herself out to safety.

Another interesting part of Mom's upbringing is that her parents, my Grandpa and Grammy Davis, would take their five kids down to Florida for the winter. They would travel down in their two old Model Ts and leave the farm in the hands of the hired help. While they were down there, they would run a grocery store in Orlando.

My mom's junior and senior years in high school, Mom rebelled from the family tradition because she hated Florida, so she stayed the winter in Windsor, Vermont with her dad's sister while attending

Windsor High School. Aunt Carrie and her husband never had children of their own and were delighted to have my mom live with them. My mom always had a special place in her heart for Aunt Carrie whom I remember as being a gentle soul. When I was very little Mom and I visited her. They had tea together. Aunt Carrie served it in a delicate tea cup and saucer. Perhaps that's why I have a collection of delicate tea cups as an adult!

I do wonder what those high school years were like for Mom though because I did hear that she was a little wild and would often want to go out, even though the adults didn't think that she should.

My parents first met at the University of Vermont when my mom had just started out in her studies as a freshman and my dad had recently returned to campus. Dad was five years older than Mom because his schooling had been interrupted by World War II.

It all started when Mom and a friend wanted to go skiing at Stowe. Back in those days, skiing was different, so people would come and pack the trails with their skis by side-stepping up the hill. Then, after a couple of hours of packing, they would get a lift ticket for the day.

"Hey," Mom's friend suggested, "you should go ask Mickey Cochran if we can get a ride with him because I know he has a car and he goes skiing a lot."

So, Mom did, and Dad was happy to drive them, and that is how my parents first met. I have no idea how either of them

THE DREAM

learned to ski or at what age they first started, but ever since they met, skiing became our family sport.

My dad was a very good athlete in general. At UVM, he was a pitcher on the baseball team and a quarterback on the football team. I remember Dad saying that he threw "a lot of junk" in baseball. I wonder if, like former Red Sox pitcher Tim Wakefield, Dad threw a lot of knuckleballs. The story was that he and Mom had already started a family when he was asked by the Boston Red Sox to try out for the team. Even though he had the skill to take on a baseball career, Dad declined because family was very important to him, and he did not want to be gone all of the time. Through that decision, Dad showed how he prioritized our family and was an amazing role model for all of us.

In 1949, Dad and Mom got married and my sister, Marilyn, was born the next year. After my parents finished up their degrees from the University of Vermont, they settled in Brownsville, Vermont, next to Mom's brother, Uncle Art.

In 1951, we moved to Dingleton Hill in Cornish, New Hampshire. I was about six weeks old. The house was a little Cape Cod-style farmhouse that hadn't been lived in for a decade until we owned it, and it had a porch that I think of as "a falling down porch." Anytime I am in a rural area today, I think about our old house because it was one of the first times I remember really connecting with rural living and noticing how much I loved it. I did always wonder about what happened to the family that had lived there before us and why they left.

Shortly after moving to Cornish, my dad became a school teacher at Windsor High School in nearby Vermont, which was also Mom's alma mater. While my dad was teaching there, the school asked him to coach baseball and skiing. The rest of the family—Bobby and Lindy—followed Marilyn and me in quick succession, with all four of us being born in a span of just three-and-a-half years.

Dad proved to be both an outstanding teacher and coach. I remember he said that his first year teaching, he was given challenging students who didn't understand math. He was able to simplify the concepts and help them overcome their fear of math. Windsor High School awarded him "Teacher of the Year."

After both my parents had passed, my sister, Marilyn, was living in the house where we grew up when a man in his late sixties stopped and shared his experience with Dad. They chatted and he told us this story:

More than fifty years prior, when he was a freshman in high school, he loved baseball, so he tried out for the team. My dad was the coach. He admitted he must have impressed Dad because not only did he make the team, but he also made varsity. He was in awe of those juniors and seniors who made up the baseball team and wasn't quite sure he could measure up. But he was thrilled to have made varsity.

When the first game came, he said that Dad must have also been impressed with his batting skills because Dad put him in the third or fourth position to bat, which is where a coach puts the best batters on the team. The first time at bat, he struck out. He felt guilty that he had let his team down. His second at-bat, he got out again.

He was mortified and went to the end of the bench to sit down away from his other teammates. Dad walked over and sat down next to him. The man told Marilyn that he didn't remember all that Dad said, but the first thing he asked him was, "Do you love baseball?" Then Dad said, "Because it doesn't look like you do." The next time at bat, this young player hit a home run!

I was so impressed hearing this story because it pointed out Dad's ability to coach. He didn't talk about technique—keeping his eye on the ball, making sure he had a level swing, or anything else that a coach might be looking for to improve his batting skills. He got him to relax and just play ball by reminding him that he really did love baseball.

Life in the Country

With Dad supporting six of us on a teacher's salary, money was tight, so Mom always had a vegetable garden. Nearby was a big blackberry patch with the juiciest, sweetest blackberries. One time, no one was home when Grammy Davis came to visit. She picked a whole bunch of blackberries and took them home to make blackberry jam, which she was planning to keep for herself.

At that point, my grandfather admonished Grammy. "No, no, no," he said, "you don't go and pick their blackberries and take them away! You have to bring them back." She didn't think we had enough money to afford sugar to make jam.

I was very young at the time, but I remember hearing that story plenty of times! After all, I was only three when my grandfather passed away from cancer. I do remember seeing him sit up in an armchair when he only had several weeks to live. I thought he was getting better because he was sitting up, but when the doctors tried to operate on him, they found out that the cancer had spread much farther than they realized.

One year, a friend of Dad's wanted to get out of raising chickens, so he gave Dad a flock of chickens and we sold eggs to make a little extra money. My mom was not crazy about the idea, but she took care of the birds and gathered, cleaned, and sorted the eggs.

Over time, we also ate some of the chickens. I remember being pretty young when my dad cut off a chicken's head. It ran around headless for a minute, and then he tied it in a tree so we could pluck it. Even though Dad was the one that plucked most of the feathers, we tried to help! Then my mom made dinner out of the fresh bird.

During the summertime, nature was our playground. Our lives were full. Mom often told us to go outside and play, so we enjoyed running around and getting into all sorts of adventures. We often had play dates with three other families who lived in Hartland, where my mom grew up. Our moms were all close friends in high school and remained close after having families.

Indeed, the Howes, the Hammonds, and the Royces became close friends to my brother and sisters, as well. I remember staying overnight with the Hammonds or Royces, or being babysat by the Howes when my parents had an event and needed someone to watch us.

One time, Marilyn, Bobby, and I, along with Andy and John Hammond, decided that we wanted to push Dad's old Doodlebug up the road so we could ride it into town. We pushed and pushed it as far as we could, but we were still very young and soon got it stuck in a big puddle! We tried to keep pushing it, but we just could not get it to go any further.

"Keep going!" one of the Hammond boys urged us on. "We can do this because I ate my Wheaties this morning!"

Unfortunately for us, but luckily for the Doodlebug, that was the end of the adventure, so we went back to playing somewhere else.

There was an old chicken coop in the back that Bobby and I (at about the ages of three and four) played in and decided that we would fix up so the rest of the family could live there, and we'd live in the big house! That idea didn't last long.

One fun thing about growing up in Cornish was that the property came with a huge barn that had several stories. It also had an old roof that was starting to fall in. My dad fixed the roof before it caved in and was able to bring it back to its magnificent, sturdy structure. I have many fond memories of playing in the barn. One of the cool things about it was that we could go in the front doors level with the road. But it was built into the hill, so once we were inside, we felt like we were upstairs with the ground a story below.

Another feature that the barn had was a hole in the floor where the previous farmers would push the manure through into a big pile. Because no one had farmed the property or even lived there for about ten years, the manure pile had sat undisturbed for that amount of time. To us, it wasn't manure; it was just a hill under the barn. One of our favorite things to do was to run through the barn, jump down through the hole, dash down the side of the pile, run around up to the road, and then do laps—run through the barn, jump down the hole, scramble down the manure, and race back up to the road and start over.

As winter approached again, Dad wanted to put up a rope-tow on the little hill next to the barn, so we could ski on our own property. He never got that project finished before he began looking for a better paying job.

Our Family Sport

As my brother and sisters and I grew up in Cornish, skiing became our family's favorite winter sport. We never thought about getting into competitions or becoming world-famous when we were young, but simply took part in skiing because we enjoyed the fun.

We learned to ski at Mount Ascutney, and we took part in the Lollipop Races that were held there every Sunday. I do not remember my first race because I was too young to recall, but I remember that one parent started the races by offering a lollipop to the winner of every age group.

I never remember winning a lollipop, but Marilyn won plenty because she was the best skier in those days. For me it was simply fun to ski on the slopes, so I did not care that much about winning.

During the week when Dad had training for his high school team, sometimes Mom would bring us over to ski for the rest of the afternoon. On weekends, we spent the day skiing. Mom would pack lunch. We never had the money to buy anything at the snack bar. How I always wished I could get a hot chocolate to warm me up!

Even though Dad was coaching the high school team, at this time, he really didn't begin training us to improve our skiing skills. We always skied on the weekend and raced in the Lollipop Races on Sunday. But there was no "training" involved for us. It was just an opportunity for us to get outside and be active skiing. That was my parents' goal. I'm sure they wanted to wear us out so we would go to bed and go to sleep—no night owls for us.

In the early fifties, all the lifts at Mt. Ascutney were rope-tows. Rope-tows were simple lifts but gave the skier a workout because it took a lot of strength to hang on to the rope while riding to the top. Mt. Ascutney even had a baby rope-tow where the hill was not very steep at all. As young kids, we could manage this rope tow because the rope was lighter and thinner. We didn't need adults or bigger kids to help us out.

One year the mountain put in a T-bar, which is a ski lift where the skier stands and is pushed up the hill by a T. Riding a T-bar is much easier than holding onto a rope, but for the little kids, it often proved more challenging.

THE DREAM

I remember one bitter, cold day, I wanted to ride the lift but needed help. To bide my time, I side-stepped up the hill a ways, skied down, and then kept repeating. I remember my feet were cold, but then I thought they warmed up. When I finally went inside, I actually began to feel my feet when they started to thaw out. They hurt so bad and felt like they were being pricked with needles. I cried because I was in such pain!

A young couple tried to give me a cup of hot chocolate to warm me up and make me feel better, but I was afraid to take it. I really wanted it, but we never bought anything from the snack bar. I thought they had bought it for themselves, and I shouldn't take it from them. Later Mom told me they had probably bought it for me. It would have been okay for me to have it. I was bummed I had missed out on such a treat!

The last year we skied at Mt. Ascutney, I broke my leg. I had mastered the snowplow and skied fast, straight down the hill with no turns. But one day on the Practice Slope, half the slope was packed, and the other half had a foot of deep, unpacked, heavy snow. As I was skiing down, the thought crossed my mind that I wondered what it would be like to ski in the deep snow. At full speed I veered into the deep, wet snow and went head over heels as my skis stopped dead.

Dad was riding up the lift and heard my bone snap, so he knew I had broken my leg. The ski patrol came and got me on a sled and brought me down to the lodge. I remember every time I tried to lift my head, excruciating pain went through my leg. I had a spiral fracture of the tibia. The ski patrol felt bad for me and promised me that they'd give me another toboggan ride after I had healed. They kept their promise, too!

When I was seven years old, Mom and Dad decided that supporting our family by teaching and coaching in the public school system just did not stretch far enough. At that point,

Dad began looking for an engineering job where he would put his college degree to good use. He soon got an interview with Boeing that was way out in the state of Washington and my parents began talking about driving all the way across the country with the four of us kids.

In the meantime, one of my uncles was working at General Electric in Burlington and told Dad that he believed there was an opening there. Dad agreed to go for an interview at GE and soon landed a job as a mechanical engineer, so we never had to try and move all the way out to Washington!

Instead, we moved out of the Cornish countryside to a little development in the suburbs of South Burlington, where we lived in a three-bedroom ranch-style house on Macintosh Avenue. The whole area had been an orchard at one point, so all the streets had apple names. We enjoyed living there for two years and had a number of great neighbors.

In Cornish, Dad accumulated tools that he needed for various tasks in the country. He seemed to have a tool for every occasion.

One day, our neighbor who lived on our street was trying to set a post and was unable to dig a proper hole for it. He finally told his wife, "Oh, go ask Mickey Cochran if he has a posthole digger!" She had no idea what a posthole digger was but went and asked Dad anyway.

Sure enough, Dad had a posthole digger! He even took time out of his own busy day to show the neighbor the best way to use the tool, but that's just how Dad was.

Dad's Big Dream

Eventually, Mom and Dad decided that it was time to move back to the country because all of us missed living in a rural area. My

THE DREAM

dad especially began talking more about making his dream of putting up a rope-tow in our very own backyard come true.

By that time, the four of us kids had started ski racing in the Northern Vermont Council, and Dad felt that it was not enough for us to only ski on the weekends. In those days, we only had the opportunity to visit the slopes on the weekends, and it was far before any ski academies even existed. After all, Dad was far ahead of his time and an excellent natural athlete himself, so he knew the importance of helping us train and practice and wanted us to be able to train and practice on weekday evenings after school so that we could become the absolute best that we could be.

At the same time, Dad had no idea that by pressing ahead with his dream that he was creating a legacy where we would become the first family of skiing and real-life Olympians! Instead, he simply knew that since everyone in his family was skiing, he wanted to give each one of us the best opportunity that we could possibly have, to "teach us a life lesson to learn to reach for a very high level of perfection and to develop the skills to where we could be quite accomplished, not so much from the winning standpoint but just to experience the hard work necessary to excel." To do that, he needed a house in the country with a hill in the backyard where he could install a rope-tow.

Eventually, my parents found a house with one hundred acres in Richmond, Vermont. It had a hill in the backyard that faced the northwest, which was perfect for skiing because it meant that the slope would hold snow throughout the winter.

I was around eight years old when I started tagging along with my parents and driving around to look at different properties in the area. There was one house that we thought was pretty cool because it came with a horse, but it didn't have a hill behind it, so it was definitely out of the question. My dad had a very clear vision of what kind of property we needed.

The ironic thing was that Mom and Dad already knew about that very same hill from many years ago. When they were attending UVM, they would take Route 2 through Richmond and see the property from across the river. My dad would see it and say, "That would make a great little ski hill someday!" but he never realized that in about ten years, he would actually own that hill and begin to develop it into our very own ski resort!

CHAPTER 2

The Skiing Cochrans

Our New Slope

We moved into our new home in September of 1960. I was nine years old. This house was a two-story Vermont farmhouse with four bedrooms. Bobby and Marilyn each had their own bedrooms, while Lindy and I shared a room. What I remember about that was that Lindy tended to be messy and I tended to be neat. We drew a line through the middle of the room where Lindy wasn't supposed to keep any of her stuff. (Today it's just the opposite—her house is neat and mine is messy)!

My parents closed on the house two weeks after school had started when we were still living in South Burlington. My mom didn't want us to have to attend the Orchard School in South Burlington for two weeks, and then move and have to switch schools, so she talked to the principal and enrolled us in Richmond. Then, for two whole weeks, Mom drove us a half hour to our new school in Richmond every morning and then made the whole trip again in the afternoon.

I remember on the first day of school in Richmond that I was very shy and that I was waiting to be taken to my new classroom. My sisters and brother were taken first, leaving me still waiting in the hall. I was finally invited to my classroom, but they did not have a desk for me yet, so I had to share with another student. The teacher put me next to a little boy named Pete who was the son of the local veterinarian and the class troublemaker, so I was not thrilled about that! Fortunately, the very next day, they had a new desk for me, and I was happy that everything was quickly figured out.

Meanwhile, Dad soon got to work on our new slope. The whole hill was wooded, so he first started out by cutting down a lot of trees. I remember one thing that we did a lot of at the beginning of the project was help Dad by dragging branches and throwing them into a huge brush pile.

At last, Dad was able to build the new rope-tow using an old tractor motor, a long length of rope, several pulleys, and strong poles. The rope was long enough that it made a complete loop, but when he was done, the two ends had to be spliced together. Marilyn remembers that she went out to help him one bitter, cold night. That was the last thing he had to do before he could start up the tow. Marilyn held a flashlight for him, so he could see. Because it was late at night and bitter cold, he didn't start the rope until the next day. Marilyn thought she should be the first to ride the lift since she helped Dad, but Bobby beat her to it. I'm not sure if she's forgiven him yet for that!

So, by February of 1961, Dad had the rope-tow going. Within another year he also had installed several powerful floodlights on the back of the house so that we could train a couple times a week after supper when it was already dark outside. In Vermont at the beginning of winter, it starts getting dark about 4:30, so if we were going to train after school, we needed to have lights. When we got home from school, we did homework, had dinner, and then skied in our backyard.

Our whole family enjoyed using our new ski slope! Even though the slope was not that long, my dad knew it was just big enough to add about 14 gates to help us with our training.

Cochran's Ski Area

In no time, the whole community found out about our ski slope and asked to join us. Ski racers within a thirty-mile radius would come train with us on Tuesday and Thursday evenings from 7PM to 10PM under our lights. From the first, my dad only had two requirements—visitors needed to chip in for gas for the rope-tow motor and take their turn being the spotter at the top of the tow.

When Dad coached athletes, he always seemed to have a magic touch when motivating them. For instance, when we were training, he always hand-timed our runs. Although he never shared this with us, one of the techniques he used when he wanted to give us a little boost was to tell us a time that was faster than we had achieved. We didn't know! We thought we had skied faster! We would get so pumped up! But when he shared this technique with another Dad, he admitted, "But I never gave them a time they weren't able to match by the end of the training session."

When Lindy was a freshman in high school, she decided that she would rather play basketball with her friends than be a ski racer. Marilyn, Bobby, and I were shocked. Skiing had become such a big part of our lives. We thought, *You have to tell Dad! How are you going to tell Dad?*

When she told him, he accepted her decision. She still went out with us on Tuesday and Thursday nights, but she didn't run the courses. Dad noticed that she skied down away from us, on the side of a trail across from where we were training. One night, he went out early and set a course right where she took her runs.

He wanted to see what she would do. He didn't say anything to her but watched her take her first run. When she got to the course, she stopped and looked at it in surprise. She stood at the start for a few minutes and then ran the course. After that, she decided she would be a ski racer after all!

Dad had an uncanny ability to inspire, motivate, and take the pressure off when coaching athletes!

On the weekends, people were happy to come out, too, and Dad charged a quarter a person for any members of the public that wanted to come and ski. Although Mom often joined us on the slopes, she stayed busy as well. She kept the kitchen nice and warm for kids who wanted to come in and get warmed up, just like an official ski lodge.

We didn't have a snack bar, although one day Mom had made a pan of brownies and left them cooling on the counter. They were going to be dessert for us later that day. But when two boys were warming up in the kitchen, the aroma got the best of them. They were just going to eat one each, but they didn't stop until they had devoured the whole pan! Decades later when my mom was in the hospital, one of the boys brought her a pan of brownies to apologize for eating the brownies when he was a young boy.

As more people came, our ski area became known far and wide as "Cochran's." Then the press began to call us "the First American Family of Skiing." It was truly incredible to look back and realize that everything was started by my parents! Even at that point, my dad didn't even think about our ski slope as a business opportunity because he was still working at GE the whole time. Instead, we all saw skiing as a hobby that we all loved and wanted to share with others. Over time, our initiatives magically transformed the entire community!

One winter day in the first year of operating the tow, a young couple in their early 20s showed up and wanted to know if they could get a real ski lesson. At the time, we didn't have a ski school or anything formal, but my dad was happy to help.

I remember him looking around at us and asking, "Is there anybody who wants to teach?"

I was around 11 years old at the time and I said, "I will!"

I had no experience in teaching, but I had been skiing for years, so I began giving the couple some hints on how to ski, how to learn the snow plow, and simple things like that. At one point, I was trying to explain the importance of keeping all their weight on the downhill ski. I could tell that they were trying to follow my instructions, but they could not quite get it. If they were making a left turn, they would push on their right ski, but their upper body weight was still on their uphill ski.

I began to get frustrated because no matter how many times I said, "You gotta get your weight on your downhill ski!" they simply could not figure it out.

Finally, I went back to my dad and said, "Dad, you know, I keep telling them they gotta get their weight on their downhill ski, but they're just not getting it! I can see that they're trying to do it, but they're just not getting it!"

Dad replied, "Sometimes, you have to say the same thing but use different words."

"What do you mean?" I asked.

With a twinkle in his eye, he suggested, "Instead of telling them to get all their weight on their downhill ski, why don't you tell them to get all their weight *off* of their uphill ski?"

"Okay," I said with a shrug and went back to the couple and told them exactly what my dad said.

Suddenly, the couple got it. It was like magic! I was ecstatic! At that moment, I learned a key lesson from my dad—sometimes, in order to get the result you are looking for, you simply have to use different words to reach it.

The other important thing that happened that day was feeling a sense of huge accomplishment. *I can teach!* I told myself, realizing that my efforts had been a great success. After that, I looked for other opportunities to help people out with their training.

Around the same time, my sisters and brother and I were continuing to improve in our own skills and soon had the opportunity to begin racing in the Northern Vermont Council. My dad was actually a key part of starting up the three ski regions in the state—Northern, Middle, and Southern. We were located in northern Vermont, so we raced against other teams from surrounding towns.

Even with our own ski slope in our backyard, we belonged to the Smuggler's Notch Ski Club. We practiced and trained with our friends on this team and raced at Stowe, Jay Peak, Glen Ellen, and Lyndonville. I raced in the Northern Vermont Council as a J4, which was a Junior aged 12 and under, and moved up to J3s when I was 13 and 14. Since Bobby and I were born in the same year, (me in January; Bob in December) we moved up the same year. We still went to the same areas as we had as J4s and raced in the same races, but the J4s and J3s won trophies for their age group. The other difference between J4s and J3s was that as a J3, a skier could qualify for the Northern Vermont Council team, which then could race against the teams from Mid-Vermont Council and Southern Vermont Council. The Middlebury Snow Bowl always held this race that we referred to as "States." Traditionally, the North was always the strongest competitors, although today skiers from throughout the state give the North a run for their money.

There's a trail that connects the top of Smuggler's Notch with the top of Big Spruce at Stowe. Usually about once a year, in the spring, we would hike the trail from Smuggler's to Stowe on our skis as an adventure. It was such a treat! Then Mom would drive around the mountain and pick us up in Stowe.

In 1964, there was a post-Olympic race at Stowe where the best racers from the U.S. were competing. I was in the 7th grade, but Mom and Dad let me and my siblings skip school so we could go watch the race. A few days later, we had a Council race at Smuggler's. I remember seeing a bunch of good racers that were from out west who skied over the mountain. I was amazed at these racers' talent! Many of them had just competed in the Olympics in Innsbruck, Austria, and they were skiing on the practice slope—OUR practice slope at Smuggler's Notch! At our awards ceremony, these incredible skiers passed out our medals. I really admired them and started dreaming about the possibilities. It was at that point that the seed was first planted in my mind that I could someday ski in the Olympics!

There was even a poster that said, "Looking for the Olympic Winner 1968." At the finish, someone asked me, Marilyn and Lindy to pose with it while someone took our picture. Each winter, we continued to practice and improve our skills. Most of all, we had a lot of fun in what we did!

At the end of that season, there was a special race called the "Quebec American" hosted by the Smuggler's Notch Ski Club where the best racers from Quebec and the Eastern U.S. could enter. I remember watching some good racers that day, but I also got to race in it, too. And I won!

The local radio station was there covering the event. They interviewed a bunch of people and aired the interviews throughout the next week. Because I won the women's race, they recorded my interview. I was excited and listened throughout the week for my interview. But it never was aired. I later found out that they couldn't use it because I had giggled too much.

I giggled a lot when I got nervous, and I was nervous! After that I made up my mind to be more composed if I ever got the chance to be interviewed again!

CHAPTER 3

The U.S. Ski Team

Skiing in High School

As a freshman in high school, skiing opened up a whole new world for me. I had grown up in Vermont and New Hampshire and visited grandparents in Maine. I had never travelled west nor had ever flown on a plane. By the time I was a freshman in high school, skiing was my family's main focus in the winter. I had school and then I had skiing.

Since we did have ski teams in high school, some people thought my siblings and I would race on the high school team, but since they didn't ski or train as much as we did, that racing level was much lower than what we were already doing, so we primarily focused on our existing training to continue to excel. I did play softball through my junior year in high school and also took part in a variety of other sports—water-skiing, hiking, swimming, biking, tennis, and soccer. Yet, skiing always remained my number one passion.

My junior and senior years in high school, I along with my brother and sister, missed a lot of school for ski racing. The best part was that everyone was very supportive of our involvement in ski racing, all the way from the students and teachers to the principal and assistant principal. In fact, they were all proud of what we were doing and could see how we were representing our whole area as athletes.

All throughout high school, as we began competing on higher levels, Dad encouraged us to do everything we could to support our abilities as ski racers. This was before health-conscious efforts became popular within the country, so he truly was ahead of his time. Dad taught us to work out and condition our bodies in order to develop strength and maintain our cardiovascular abilities. Several times a week, we lifted weights, jogged, and performed regular stretches.

One thing I remember that prompted Dad to be ahead of his time was because of a story of a prominent ski racer from the 1950s. Her name was Jill Kinmont and she fell during a race in Utah and broke her neck. As a result, she became paralyzed for life from the shoulders down. My dad took that story to heart and did his best to make sure that we would be as strong as we could be. He would especially emphasize to us that we needed to protect certain critical parts of our bodies, such as our joints and our necks.

Ever since I was 13 years old, Dad started coaching us on how to strengthen our bodies.

"How many pushups can you do?" Dad would challenge us, getting down on the floor with us and showing us how to do it right.

Then he made a chart for each of us so that we could keep track of our exercises and how many repetitions we could do. Our schedule was to try and work out for two days in a row and take the third day off to allow our muscles to heal.

It was not until much later that I realized how unusual Dad's methods were for the time. Even on the higher team levels, there were very few athletes that participated in such intentional conditioning. I remember one teammate, Karen Budge from Jackson Hole, Wyoming, who said that her dad felt that she should be working out. He would drive her out of town and drop her off, telling her to run back home, but she did not like doing that at all and pretty much refused to work out!

At our summer camps, we did have some conditioning methods, but it was nothing like how things are today. Today, athletes are constantly working out, looking into all of the scientific research, testing their lactose levels, and much more. As I think back on my own history, it makes me all the more appreciative of my dad's knowledge and how he instructed us in our training.

When I was a freshman, Marilyn was a sophomore and Bob was in 8th grade, but all three of us were J2s. That meant that we were no longer racing against only the northern Vermont racers, but any competitor from the East that was fifteen years old or older. Even though by age we were categorized as J2s, we also competed against J1s and didn't receive recognition for winning at the J2 level. It also meant that our races were qualifiers to make "States." If we did well enough, we would be members of the Vermont State team and race at Easterns against the other state teams from the Northeast.

Bobby's and my first year as a J2 was actually Marilyn's second year. Looking back, I realize that Dad's coaching methods taught us many lessons about having confidence in ourselves and keeping a mental focus in order to succeed. As a natural result, all of us thought that we could win. Marilyn did so well her first year in J2s that she qualified for Junior Nationals in Bend, Oregon. Dad flew out with her. I remember him calling home after her races. I asked Mom, "Did she win?" She didn't, but I believed she could have, even against the best juniors from all of the U.S.

The next year, Bobby and I moved up to J2s. During that progression, I knew that Marilyn, Bobby, and I were some of the best skiers in the State, so it did not surprise me when all three of us made the Eastern Team to race at Junior Nationals in

Winter Park, Colorado. Dad was chosen to be the coach. It was the first time I had been west of Vermont and the first time I had flown on a plane. I won the giant slalom and Marilyn won the slalom. Another Vermont girl, Erica Skinger, won the downhill.

I also remember being in awe of the new experience. I also was quite naïve. When we gathered for breakfast the first morning, we were served pancakes. Coming from Vermont, I was hoping they would have true maple syrup, rather than the fake kind like Aunt Jemima. One of the girls on our team told us, "Out here they don't have maple syrup—they have sequoia syrup!" I totally believed her! She later told us the only kind of tree she could think of was sequoia, so that's what she told us.

The other thing I remember from that race was that a lot of the westerners were complaining about the icy conditions. We easterners on the other hand, looked around and wondered, *Where's the ice?* We thought the snow conditions were perfect!

We were proud to come from the East. In those days, we would say, "If you want to learn to be the best skier, then learn how to ski in the East!" After all, we were often faced with some of the harshest weather conditions. I remember one race at Stowe where I put two blankets over my head to protect me from the severe wind chill. Because the chairlifts could be bitterly cold, Stowe provided blankets for the ride. This one race was a downhill, which is the longest run at the fastest speed, which I never particularly liked.

I remember being at the top of the hill in the first aid hut and there was a group of us huddled together trying to stay warm while we were waiting for the coaches to decide whether or not they were actually going to host the race. The wind chill that day was a dramatic -70° F and they eventually cancelled it. By contrast, other days it would get so warm that it would begin to rain instead of snow. But then the weather would change, and the temperatures would drop so we would end up skiing on ice! There's a saying in Vermont that if you don't like the weather, just wait five minutes!

The U.S. Ski Team

In our last several years of high school, as my sisters, brother, and I continued to race, we rose pretty quickly to the top of the national level and were soon qualified to make the U.S. Ski Team.

In thinking back to that whole period of time, it was always amazing for me to look back and realize that my whole family was part of the history of skiing in the U.S. At the time, the U.S. Ski Team was not very well established, and the coaches were still figuring out how their process should work. For instance, when selecting the 1968 Olympic Team, the final names were picked in April of 1967.

Prior to the Junior Nationals in Winter Park, Colorado in 1966, to make the U.S. Ski Team, a racer had to be ranked in the top ten in an event (downhill, slalom, or giant slalom) in the nation. There were no other levels. But after the Junior Nationals in which Marilyn, Erica, and I won, the national coaches added a "Hopeful Squad." Today, we probably would have been referred to as a development team or the B-Team. As I recall, they explained, "You are now part of the team, but not really!" Whatever that meant!

Ironically, even though we were put in a lower category, we were actually so good that we gave the main U.S. Ski Team a run for their money! In August of 1967, the "Hopefuls" were invited to train in Chile with the rest of the U.S. Ski Team. We were young and full of energy. We actually came up with a song that mimicked the Monkees', "Hey, Hey, We're the Monkees!" Our song went something like this: "Hey! Hey!

We're the Hopefuls! We don't mess around, we're too busy winning, to put anybody down!"

At the time, I was grateful to be part of the Hopefuls and grateful for the opportunity to train in South America under winter conditions during our summer months. I didn't realize that the established members of the ski team felt threatened by our appearance.

In December of 1967 at our training camp in Aspen, Colorado, another three girls were picked to go to Europe to race in the World Cup, which was also a brand-new series of races that had only been in existence for a year. Some people thought that I should have been the third girl to be picked, but I was actually very glad that I was not chosen to go. I was only 16 at the time, had never been to Europe, and had limited travel experience outside of New England except to go to several different training camps. In addition to that, I was not a very sophisticated person at all and not looking for any kind of fame, so I was simply happy not to be chosen.

Meanwhile, based on the results of the World Cup races, the selections for the Olympics suddenly changed. Two of the three girls that had been sent to Europe and raced in the World Cup in January 1968 did very well for themselves. Even though they did not make the original Olympic list that past April, the coaches decided that those two girls should replace two of the original girls who had already been selected for the Olympics. Everything was done in such a way that the first two girls felt very rudely booted off of the team. The second two girls really were skiing better than the original two girls, but there was a lot of bitterness about the whole way the situation was handled for quite some time.

Then there were other things about the evolving U.S. Ski Team that were much different than today. The veteran members of the ski team shared that in the past, when they travelled to Europe for the races, the team only had enough money to buy one-way tickets, so the coaches would tell the competitors, "We'll figure out how to get money to bring you back home later."

In the meantime, I remained on the "Hopeful Squad" until they formed a B-Team and an A-Team and became more organized. Marilyn made the A-Team first, and then I soon followed along that same season.

During my senior year of high school, another exciting series of events happened during the spring FIS races that took place out West. We had a couple different kinds of ski races, but my favorite had always been slalom. I could do okay with the others, but I didn't really expect to win them. The first race was a giant slalom. I drew number one and I won, so I was excited about that!

Back in those days, the start order was drawn by seeds of fifteen. The number selection process was set up in a type of slot-machine system that had all the racing numbers in one box and all the names in another. As each group of racers came up, they would select a number from the machine and then a name from the other bin. Because I was in the first seed, I knew I would start somewhere in the top fifteen. But when number one popped up, my name popped up from the second box.

At the next race, I drew number one again, and won that one as well! From then on, at every FIS giant slalom race that we attended for the spring series, I continued to draw number one and win them. I was starting to wonder about the machine pattern and if the whole system was rigged! At the same time, from then on, no matter what level I was skiing in, I always loved whenever I drew a number one because it gave me that little extra boost of confidence. History convinced me that when I started first, I had a good chance of winning!

My dad even became Director of the Alpine Ski Team in 1973 for the '73-'74 season and took a leave of absence from General

Electric to focus on coaching. Looking back, our time on the U.S. Ski Team was relatively short because Marilyn, Bob, and I all retired from ski racing by 1974, but our adventures were jam-packed with excitement the entire time.

Advancing to the Olympics

As I continued to do well in all of my races and advance throughout the different levels, there was no question in my mind that I would race on a global level in the World Cup. By 1970, Marilyn, Bob, and I all reached the World Championships where we competed for the U.S. Four years later, Lindy joined us in the World Championships, so all of us Cochran kids represented the U.S. in 1974. In between that, Marilyn, Bob, and I all competed in the Olympics in 1972, with Lindy later on making the Olympics in 1976.

When I was selected for the Olympics in 1972, it seemed like such a natural process of events that I did not respond with a lot of surprise. All of us Cochrans were considered to be the U.S.'s best chance at gaining a medal in any event. In fact, I was ranked one of the top slalom skiers in the world. So, in that sense, it never dawned on me that I would *not* be on the team because I knew that I belonged there!

Later on, when I did win the gold medal in the Olympics, my results took a lot of people by surprise. Once again, I was not surprised at all, since I knew I had the talent and the skills to win, and that I could ski with the best of them. I truly belonged right there in the winners' circle with all of the other champions! The most unexpected thing for me after winning the Olympic gold was actually how shocked everyone else was that I won!

It all started in 1967 at the training camp in Aspen, Colorado, which was the same year that different people thought I should be selected for the World Cup races in Europe, while

I was simply glad not to go. In the summer of 1968, I went for another training camp in Chile and then began my senior year in high school. By that December, I was selected to go to Europe to compete in the World Cup and I finally felt ready for my next adventure.

I remember arriving in Val d'Isère, France, that first weekend in December and looking all around me in wonder at the new sights and sounds. Ever since I was a little girl, I always was a tremendous daydreamer, sometimes even staring out the window at school and getting lost in my own thoughts.

This time in Europe, I began daydreaming one morning and asking myself all sorts of questions as I was getting ready for the day. *What is it that makes the Europeans such good skiers?* I thought. *How are they different from me and other Americans? What makes them so much better?*

As I wondered about all of these things, I was sitting down and began pulling on my ski pants. Suddenly a surprising thought came to me: *They're not better than I am! They put their ski pants on the same way I do. We all put in one leg at a time!*

With this great epiphany burning in my mind, I no longer felt as intimidated to be in Europe as I had first been. I finally realized that I was just as talented as the best European skier and that I had just as good a chance at winning! I kept that same attitude with me in the years that followed as I continued to do well in the races and soon reached the Olympics in 1972.

Before we knew it, Marilyn, Bobby, and I were in Sapporo, Japan, getting ready for our big day at the Winter Games. We were both excited and wondering about the possibilities of one of us winning. The evening before the women's slalom race, we were talking with a Japanese family who were friends with my grandma. They wanted to take us out to dinner while we were in the area, so we were trying to make arrangements with them.

As it turned out, the family hoped to take us out the evening *after* the race, but then the question came up once again, "What happens if one of you wins—either you or Marilyn? Will it still work to have dinner?"

Both Marilyn and I knew that it was very possible that one of us could win, but we both looked at each other and said, "Oh, no, we'll still go!" So, there were our dinner plans.

In the meantime, we knew that we would be racing at Mount Teine in the morning, so we made sure to get plenty of rest that night and be ready for the big day.

My Big Day

The next morning, Marilyn and I woke up, got dressed, ate breakfast, and then began to get all our gear together so that we could load it all up on the bus that would take us up the mountain. I was a little superstitious because I had a favorite scarf that I would always wear for good luck, so I made sure to put that around my neck as we were getting ready to go.

During the thirty-minute bus ride up to Mount Teine where the events were being held, I kept myself occupied by continuing to read a novel called *Hawaii* by James Michener. The first 100 pages had been a pretty slow read, but now that I was into the good part, I was hardly able to put it down during the whole trip up the mountain.

In no time, we all arrived at the base of the mountain. We had already drawn our numbers and I had number one, so of course I was happy about that. My coach was also really excited because he knew how much I favored that number. From there, I took my time in walking the course, or hiking from the bottom of the course all the way up to the top so I could carefully memorize each part and think about each gate.

Once I reached the top, I looked back and visualized how I would ski down and what it would take for me to reach the finish. It always took some time because I had to recognize for each gate, *Open gate, open gate, flush, open, open, hairpin, quick turns, set up here, let my skis run here,* and so on. At the same time, I had become so experienced in memorizing and visualizing an entire course that, when I finally reached the top, I could turn around and draw out a map to explain exactly where the gates were and what it would take to complete the whole race.

The most important part in memorizing the course was always in knowing what gates were at the very bottom because they were the easiest to mess up. For instance, if a course had 45 to 50 gates, by the time a skier reached the bottom, they would already feel tired, and that last stretch would be where it was easiest to mess up.

For me, however, because I was working up the course backwards in my mind, by the time I reached the top, I had already visualized going through the last gates at least 30 or 35 times. I truly have my dad to thank for becoming so good at that, since he encouraged all of us to always memorize every single course before we went down it.

Finally, I reached the top and the races were about to get started. By this time, I was fully in the zone. I had studied the course, memorized each of the gates, and practiced skiing it in my head. I was completely tuned into myself and had shut everybody else out around me. I didn't talk to anyone else or joke around with them. Instead, I was fully concentrating on myself as I did some stretches and mild exercises to get my blood flowing.

As I got closer to the start, I practiced visualizing the course again. Soon, it was time to hand my parka and warmups to the coach. I always wore mittens, even though many racers preferred to wear gloves because they thought they could feel their poles

HIKE THE COURSE

better. For me, I always figured that since mittens kept my hands warmer, if my hands were freezing, then I wouldn't feel my poles anyway! Then my coach helped rub my legs to make sure that I was loose and ready to go.

As I slid into position for the first run, I was presented with an unexpected challenge—the clock! I couldn't figure out when I should go because it didn't look like a regular clock. I remember staring at that strange clock in bewilderment. It was pure white with one black slash on it, but it had no numbers and only one hand that rotated around the clock. I simply could not figure it out! I thought it would let off a series of beeps to let me know when to go. Meanwhile, the forerunners were leaving ahead of me, so I figured that I would just wait until it beeped down and then I would know when to go.

At the time, I was 5'1" and the start of the course was slightly tilted backwards, so that was another thing that made it difficult for me. Most of the time, I would try to lean back, almost as if I was getting ready to sit down in a chair, and then start the race by pushing up and lunging forward as fast as I could. The start was always the slowest part of the course since we had to go from zero and get up to speed as quickly as possible.

Meanwhile, I was carefully in position and focused on the clock, waiting for it to beep or count down. All of a sudden, it beeped once, but there was nothing else. I hesitated for a second, a million thoughts rushing through my head.

Only one beep? What's going on here? Am I supposed to go or not? How am I supposed to know?

I knew that I only had one second to spare on either side of the start signal, so I plunged ahead and started the course, hoping that my timing was right as I focused on the race before me.

As I struggled to get up to speed, I still had several other worrying thoughts flash through my mind: *Am I going to be disqualified for leaving early or late? It's electric timing, so my time will be accurate, but should I stop and try to get a rerun to make sure?*

That last question was easy for me to answer. *No! I probably won't get a rerun and that will be the end of the Olympics for me. Just keep going!*

So, I put all of those thoughts aside and kept going, coming to the finish line in no time and winning it by three-hundredths of a second! I knew that I had a second run to get in for that race, so I was on to memorizing and visualizing the next course.

As I was hiking up the second course, about halfway up, I ran into a Canadian girl named Kathy Kreiner whose hands were freezing. She had gloves on that clearly were not working for her.

I said, "Oh, my hands are so warm. Let's trade—you wear my mittens to get your hands warmed up and I'll wear your gloves to warm them up. Then we'll trade once we're at the top."

So, that's what we did. I had raced her and a lot of the other skiers before, so some of us had become friends. Ironically, after I won the Olympic gold, I heard that the sale of mittens went up!

In the meantime, I was still working on memorizing the course for the second run, but I could feel myself starting to choke because I started to think about all sorts of things. First of all, I was daydreaming about what it would be like to win a gold medal because I had already won that first run.

I was wondering, *What do I have to do to stay ahead of these other girls?* I started thinking, *I hope I don't make any mistakes! I hope I don't fall! I hope—* and my mind was just going crazy with the results that I wanted to get. I could feel myself getting tighter and tenser, which made my mind spin even more. *Oh no! I'm going to choke! I don't want to choke. What do I have to do not to choke?*

Finally, I caught myself and realized that too much nonsense was going on in my head. *B.A.*, I told myself, *You've got to change how you're thinking because, right now, this is not working.*

So, I grabbed ahold of several thoughts that would help me. First, I thought, *All you can ask of yourself is to just put your best effort into it. That's it!*

My second thought was, *You know, if the French girls can win, I can too!* In fact, I had been reflecting on that exact same thought the night before and realized, *Somebody has to win, so why can't that somebody be me?* That made me even more determined to try my best.

My third thought was something that my dad had told me at the World Championships two years prior. He said, "I always thought you were the 'cool cucumber' in the family." I felt a rush of relief and told myself, *I'm the 'cool cucumber' in the family!*

Finally, my fourth thought was what really released the pressure for me. I said to myself, *Listen, you've won the first run of an Olympic slalom race. So, no matter what happens in the second run, not many people have done what you've just done. No matter what happens, you can always be proud of what you've already accomplished!*

After that, I was ready to concentrate on the course and finish getting ready for the second run. Most of all, I was determined to figure out the clock and get a better start. I felt that I needed to be close to the wand but also needed to have some space to launch myself out of the starting position.

As it turned out, what happened was that when I started to sit back in my imaginary chair to lunge forward, my knees went forward and opened the wand a little early. I got out onto the course easily enough, but I knew that I had lost some time because of the way I had started off. Just like the first start, however, I knew that once it happened, it was already over with. So, I just put it in the back of my mind and tried to forget about it. I had to focus on skiing the best that I could for the second run!

And that is exactly what I did. When I finished, I found out that I lost that run by one-hundredth of a second, but that I had won overall by two-hundredths! The other interesting part of it was that all of the girls who were possibly able to beat me for the second run went ahead of me. The French skier, Danièle Debernard, was one of them. She had been three-hundredths of a second behind me on the first run, but she beat everybody else by a full second on the second run!

That was a huge accomplishment for Danièle, but I was completely unaware of it at the time. In fact, I didn't care to know because I didn't want to watch her or anybody else. I had my own plan on how I was going to take the course for the second run. I focused on doing my same routine—stretch, exercise, visualize the course, and be ready to start. Most of all, I told myself, *Just do the best that you can!*

When I reached the end of the run, my brother and boyfriend were waiting for me. There was a fence at the bottom, and they jumped over it and ran over to me, putting me up on their shoulders. In that moment, that's when I knew that I had won. It's funny, though, because Bob told me afterwards that it was hard to see the scoreboard and they actually didn't even look at the time. They did not know that I had won!

When I asked Bob for clarification, he said, "No, we didn't know. We were just so happy that you finished the race!"

That evening, we went to the big ceremony where they gave out the medals. We had to wait until the figure skating competition was over and then they had a whole line-up of awards for a bunch of different events.

The hardest part for me was actually getting up in front of everybody and receiving my medal. In fact, standing at the starting gate and taking my runs was the easiest part of the whole day! I simply did not like being in front of everybody, having everybody stare at me, and feeling like the center of attention. My worst fear of all was having to walk up on that big stage and then accidentally tripping and falling with my pants splitting open so everyone could see my underwear!

One thing I was looking forward to seeing, however, was what I remembered from two years back when I had won a silver medal at the World Championships. The ceremonies were similar since they both called us up to the podium and they have different flags displayed to show what countries are being represented by the three winners. Whoever won the event would have their flag raised the highest and then the national anthem from that country would be played during the ceremony.

When the moment came, it was really special for me to hear "The Star-Spangled Banner" and see the U.S. flag flying high up on the podium. Two years before that, we had listened to the French national anthem and watched the French flag being raised into the highest position since one of the French skiers had won. I had a huge rush of mixed feelings that night. On the one hand, I was trying to control my emotions since I knew that a lot of people were watching me. At the same time, I was feeling very proud, smiling a lot, and even raising my hands above me in victory. It was such an amazing conclusion to my big day!

CHAPTER 4

The Legacy

Passing on the Torch

By 1974, Marilyn, Bob, and I knew that it was time to retire. At the time, Marilyn was 24, I was 23, and Bob was 22. I felt like the U.S. Ski Team had had enough of the Cochrans. Lindy was only 20 and continued to race as a member of the U.S. Ski Team for another four years.

1974 was the year that Dad was the Alpine Ski Director. When he had been offered the job, he talked to our family and wondered how we all felt if he took the job. Marilyn was concerned because she knew he wasn't a politician and could be facing some adverse conditions.

I was ecstatic! I knew how great a coach he was and was thrilled that my teammates would also be able to experience his coaching. He had already built up a lot of experience in coaching the ski team at the University of Vermont and bringing their skiers up to a professional level, so I thought he could help both the U.S. athletes and coaches get even better—maybe even dominate the World Cup.

What I didn't realize was that some of my teammates weren't sure that Dad could coach fairly. Some felt that he would favor his own kids. After all, all four of us were racing at the World Cup level!

But I never experienced that. I knew that he wanted each athlete to develop to the best of his ability. He was very conscious of not showing us favoritism. An example of that was when he coached the Eastern team for the Junior Nationals in 1966. He placed another Eastern racer in the start order ahead of me in the giant slalom. He told me, "I'm putting you in the 3rd start position for the East because I don't want anyone to think I'm playing favorites. I know you could be 2nd, but I'm putting you 3rd." I understood and had no problem with it. Even though I started 24th, I still won the race.

With Dad's background in science and math, he analyzed skiing through scientific concepts. He realized that ski racers were nothing more than "bodies in motion," so the principles in physics would also apply to skiers. I remember him using terms like "vectors" and "inertia" to explain technique.

Looking back, I don't think the U.S. Ski Team was ready for his methods. Dad's dream was really to educate the other coaches and incorporate his scientific methods into coaching the racers. They were ideas that the other coaches had never heard of before and were not very receptive to.

Around the same time, there was a young girl who became the high hopes of the U.S. Ski Team, almost like a Mikaela Shiffrin of today. Although she was good, she didn't turn out to be an Alpine skiing phenomenon. Over the years, there definitely have been some amazing skiing sensations, including Bode Miller, Lindsey Vonn, Julia Mancuso, Ted Ligety, and of course Mikaela Shiffrin.

My dad's focus, however, was never on just developing one individual out of the pack but on strengthening the Team as a whole. Although the U.S. Ski Team has shifted back and forth from embracing more of a team philosophy to catering to a superstar, the trustees love when U.S. skiers win and favor an individual over the team concept.

The other thing that happened around the time of our retirement was that we were going through a family emergency. In early January 1974, Marilyn, Lindy, Dad, and I were in Pfronten, Germany for a couple of World Cup races with the rest of our team. One night, we all went to bed, and everything seemed very normal and ordinary. In the morning, when we three girls woke up, Dad was gone! No one seemed to know where he was and what had happened to him.

What actually happened was that my mom had suffered a nervous breakdown back home in Vermont. She had been trying to run the ski area on her own that winter, but since she usually struggled with seasonal depression because of the decrease of light during the dark winter days, it became even more difficult for her.

One day, she was cleaning up the kitchen. She had hired one of my high school classmates to help her with the house chores. Lisa was upstairs vacuuming when my mom heard on the radio that five members of an American family were all killed in a plane crash in Italy.

Immediately, Mom felt deep inside that she had lost her entire family. She just knew that it had to be all of us! Almost instantaneously, she dropped to the floor, lost the feeling in her legs, felt like she was paralyzed from the waist down, and began screaming and crying uncontrollably.

As it turned out, Mom had a mental and nervous breakdown, so she was taken to the psychiatric ward for treatment. The doctor called up Dad in the middle of the night and told him what happened, saying, "You really need to come home immediately."

That was why Dad suddenly left. He did tell the other coach that he was rooming with what had happened and where he was going, but the coach probably wasn't fully awake, so he didn't really remember what Dad said.

That whole season was a difficult time for all of us because Mom was so depressed. In fact, the last two years that I was racing, I felt like I wanted to get hurt so I could stop racing. I wanted to take a break, but I didn't want to make that decision outright. If I got hurt, the decision would be made for me. I wasn't quite ready to retire, but the energy of the whole sport had declined for me in quite a few ways.

I remember seeing problems in my relationships with some other athletes during that time as well. For instance, one of my teammates was frustrated with her own skiing and questioned Dad's coaching. She was struggling with downhill and felt that my dad wasn't helping her in the way that she expected him to, so she started to lose her faith in his coaching abilities.

She said something to me about it at one point and I responded by saying, "Maybe you need to take a look at your own skiing first." I was trying to explain that instead of pointing the finger at my dad that she should take a look inside herself first to see what was going on. Cindy did not like my response, however, so I always felt like there were some bad feelings between us after that.

Overall, when the time finally came, I was fully ready to retire. I came home and then ended up going back to college so I could finish up my degree after many years. Even though I had graduated from high school in 1969, I did not go to school that fall because that winter was a World Championship year. In the fall of 1970, I took one semester at the University of Vermont, but then I was focused on skiing for the next year-and-a-half. If it was a World Championship year or an Olympic year, then I wouldn't go to school in the fall before the season started, but when there was an in-between year, I would take a semester of studies. After retiring, I was finally able to focus on finishing up my degree in home economics education with a minor in health.

The year after I retired, I coached the women's ski team at the University of Vermont, which was a fun job. It also came with its own challenges because I noticed how much of a difference there was between the men and women's athletic departments. While the Men's Athletic Director was focused on the competition of the sport and making sure the athletes became the best that they could be, the Women's Athletic Director was not so concerned about being competitive and seemed to be more interested in making sure that the girls were having fun. Of course, the female coaches were very nice, but they seemed to be threatened that I would focus only on being competitive, at whatever cost. I didn't care if we won or lost, as long as each athlete put in their best effort. I wanted the women to improve and do the best they could. It wasn't important to me that they be the best.

In fact, the women administrators were a little concerned when I was hired because they thought that I might try and make the girls be just as competitive as I had been and as competitive as the guys. I was not hoping to change everything and force the girls to be competitive, but at the same time I did want them to strive toward doing the best that they could do. As I watched all the dynamics that were going on and the differences between the men's and women's teams, I thought that it was very strange based on where I had been in the world.

The other thing that struck me during that time was the difference in finances between the men's and women's divisions. Since I was still in school, I asked if my tuition could be covered as part of my coaching contract, but the women's division responded with a clear, "No."

At the same time, however, I watched as the men's division worked out a deal with a local baseball player to coach the baseball team while covering some of his tuition! The compensation for the men's UVM baseball coach was $7,000, while I was just getting $2,000 to coach the women's ski team. Even though there was an enormous pay difference, I also recognized that the women's division had a much different attitude, treating skiing more like funding games instead of actually developing skills and playing a real sport between professional-level athletes.

Today, the attitude at UVM is much different and the athletes can be spotted a mile away because of their true dedication to the sport. Instead of having separate athletic departments, they have combined them into one and have the same coaches. The young people are also very determined to do their best! Whenever I visit my alma mater, these athletes talk about their hopes to make their national teams and work their way into skiing in the Olympics. It is amazing to see how the aspirations for sports have grown and developed over the years—a stark contrast to what I experienced in my own college days!

New Opportunities

The next several years were dedicated to finishing school, getting married, doing some substitute teaching, and instructing at Cochran's. By that time, our family ski area had expanded and was more established. Over the years, my parents bought more land, built another rope-tow, T-bar, Mighty-Mite, a new lodge and then a newer lodge, added a snack bar, more trails, and gave ski lessons. While my parents were alive, it still could be classified as a mom-and-pop operation but had developed a following of dedicated families who were proud to be from Cochran's.

As the years continued, I became more involved in another one of my true passions—teaching. I especially enjoyed when the two of them came together! After I had retired from ski racing, I was approached by a former U.S. Ski Team teammate named Steve Lathrop who ran adult racing camps, some at Waterville Valley in New Hampshire and another in Pennsylvania. He asked me if I would coach so I helped out coaching at his camps for a time.

In both of my marriages, I knew that I needed to have those men in my life at the particular stage I was in. My first husband that I married in 1977 was a school teacher whom I admired. His students loved him. I was hoping I would become as loved by my students once I graduated from college and began teaching myself.

Ron also loved politics and making an impact on educational policies. He became president of the Vermont National Education Association and then landed a job with the Student NEA in Washington, DC. At that point, we moved to Virginia for two and a half years until he decided to go to law school in Vermont and we moved back home. During the winters, I returned to Vermont to teach the week-long ski lessons during December and February school vacations.

Later, while my husband was in law school, I began my first teaching job at the Winooski School District where I taught health in Grades 1-6 and Home Economics for Grades 7 and 8. I was there for one year and it was quite an interesting experience.

For instance, after I was hired and before I took over the former teacher's classes, I hoped to talk to her and gain any tips from her that she might be willing to pass on. She had already left, but I was able to meet her at her house one afternoon.

She greeted me at the door with the strangest introduction that I could expect from a fellow teacher. "I just thought you should know that you weren't the first pick from the committee," she said. Not pausing to hear a response from me, she went on, "You weren't even the second or the third one to be picked, but more like the fifth!"

I felt mad about the way she said all of that, wondering why she would be so mean to tell me all that in the way she did. I came to realize that the people in the committee were narrow-sighted because they felt like they had to answer this question regarding hiring me: "Do we want a teacher in our school, or do we want an athlete?"

Often, I had to face people who were convinced that, because I had been an athlete at the highest level, it suddenly meant that I couldn't also be a teacher! At the same time, I have always felt like it was my purpose in life to be a teacher, despite what athletic accomplishments I have gained. Unfortunately, not everyone felt that way about me.

While I was at Winooski, I was also asked to be the J.V. field hockey coach. I didn't know a lot about field hockey except that there were eleven players on the field, which was like soccer. I had never played field hockey or even seen a game of field hockey, but I figured the strategies would be a lot like soccer. So I said, "Yes! I'd love to coach field hockey!"

The first thing I did was to take a book out from the library to learn the rules and see what the equipment was like. I had no idea what the ball was like or the stick. When I learned that an athlete could only hit the ball on one side of the stick, I thought, *There's some silly rules in field hockey!*

Luckily for me, there were not enough girls to make up a J.V. team, so I became the assistant coach to the Varsity coach. She was fantastic! I learned so much from her and I was able to instill some motivation and belief in the players that anything was possible. Winooski had never done well enough to make playoffs, but that year we did. I like to think that maybe I had a small part in helping our team achieve that!

After teaching in Winooski for one year, the job was cut from full-time to part-time, so I began looking for other teaching opportunities. During that transition, I also went through a divorce with my first husband. I eventually ended up working at Spaulding High School in Barre, Vermont where I taught for six years.

I loved my new job at Spaulding because of the great people that I worked alongside. Again, I was asked to coach J.V. field hockey. What I was realizing, was that as much as I enjoyed teaching, I loved coaching even more. One year I was also asked to coach track and field. Even though it wasn't my expertise, I enjoyed coaching and learning about the different events. I coached the girls' high jump and long-distance running.

Our first meet fell during spring vacation, and we were hosting. One of the teams at the meet included the best long-distance runner in the state. When one of my athletes came to me, she was excited because she had found out that that athlete wasn't there because she was on a European school trip. Ann thought she could win the mile! I told her, "Ann, you should be disappointed that she's not here! You could race against the best in the state. What if you actually won the race—how great would that be? Even if you didn't win, by racing against someone better than you, you could have your personal best. And that would be a win in and of itself! There's a lot to be gained by competing against the best that are around! Accept the challenge of a better competitor!"

In the meantime, my sisters and brother were also taking their own paths in different directions. Marilyn got married in 1978. Bob retired from the U.S. Ski Team, raced pro for a couple years before going to medical school, and then got married in 1979. Lindy continued to race in the World Cup and Olympics for four years, and then went to UVM and skied for them. She met her future husband when she joined a tennis club and was introduced to him by a mutual friend. They got married in 1980.

By the time I was in my mid-thirties, I yearned to have a family of my own. My siblings had children and I loved spending time with them, but I felt like there was an empty ache inside of me without having my own kids. Growing up, I loved babies and loved taking care of kids. When I was little, I thought I wanted a dozen children. As I got older, I thought it would be great to have six. But by my mid-thirties, I wasn't sure if I'd ever have any.

I dated another teacher off and on when I was at Spaulding who had a young daughter. His wife had died of cancer the year before I started teaching there and I felt like I was a mom to Hannah. I adored her, and it was hard when we eventually broke up. When I was married to my first husband, I had suffered a couple of miscarriages and was beginning to despair that I would never have children of my own.

But then my best friend from high school introduced me to Drew, who had just moved next door with his daughter. We met in January and got married in June. By then, I was in my late thirties and felt that my biological clock was ticking down. I also knew that both my parents were growing older, so my greatest concern was that I wanted healthy babies and that they would get to know their grandparents and have a meaningful relationship with them.

After having miscarriages, I wasn't sure if I'd be able to have kids, but by October I found out that I was pregnant. When I was 39, I gave birth to my daughter, Caitlin, on my sister Lindy's birthday, and then my son, Ryan, was born two years later. When they were young, I got divorced the second time. After two failed marriages, I felt that I did not need to have a man in my life anymore. At that point, I was a part-time teacher and working at Cochran's on the weekends, so I felt that I could handle everything, pay the bills, and focus on raising my children.

The Grandchildren

As my brother and sisters and I had kids and they all began to grow up, the Cochran grandchildren learned to ski on our family hill and developed their own love for the sport. My kids, Caitlin and Ryan, had almost no choice because I always worked at Cochran's on the weekends. At that point, Dad's old rope-tow behind the house no longer ran, but everything was much more professional and continued to grow over the years.

The skiing journey for my kids was a bit different than for the other ski racers in the country partly because mine were the youngest out of all the Cochran cousins and had cousins who had been successful at the national and international level. We also had the added challenge that I did not have the money to send them to expensive camps—for instance, to South America—over the summer like some parents do once their children reach their early teens. Instead, I encouraged both Caitlin and Ryan to play other sports and develop their interests in other areas instead of just skiing.

My family was a tremendous help in outfitting my kids. They inherited hand-me-downs from their older cousins from suits to equipment, since I didn't have the money to outfit them. My family also helped out financially so they could go to ski camps organized and coached by Lindy at Sunday River in Maine and Mt. Hood in Oregon. When Ryan made World Juniors and World Championships, my siblings and brother-in-law made sure I could go and paid for my trips.

In Caitlin's case, she was just as incredible as any of the other Cochran grandchildren, learning how to ski at a young age and even winning a number of races. At the same time, she preferred not to focus on skiing, partly because she felt that she was never good enough to be a "Skiing Cochran" and that she was unable to fully relate to the skiing emphasis of the whole family. She actually connected more with some of her cousins who shared her feeling of not fully fitting into the sport, instead of being fully passionate about skiing like her brother, Ryan.

In her own way, however, Caitlin has always been dedicated to Cochran's. For example, she has talked about helping with the marketing side of the business because of her strong background in sales. In addition to that, her two young children are already beginning to take part in the skiing classes!

For Ryan, he absolutely loved the sport and worked hard to improve his skills all throughout high school. Around his graduation, when he was 18 years old, I distinctly remember receiving an email on May 26th from the U.S. Ski Team that stated, "Congratulations! Ryan Cochran-Siegle has been nominated for the Development Team of the U.S.A Team!"

Before I could get too excited, I read the next line: "If he decides to accept this nomination, please send $5,000 by June 1st."

I had to laugh in disbelief at that point because we were living paycheck-to-paycheck and there was no way that I had an extra $5,000 just lying around to send to the U.S. Ski Team! In fact, I further discovered that it would cost Ryan a total of $20,000 to be part of the Team because that was how they were raising money for their program at that time. This was definitely not the way that things worked when I first started racing.

As I continued to look into it, I found out why they were charging so many costs. The U.S. Ski Team built a training center in Park City, Utah, called The Center of Excellence, which had an incredible amount of annual taxes because they failed to set it up properly as a non-profit organization. The COE, known as the Center of Excellence, is restricted to U.S. Ski Team members only, and the public is not allowed to use the facility. I believe that may have been why they still had to pay property taxes based on a for-profit business, since true non-profits are not allowed to exercise that kind of exclusivity.

It was such a huge change from when I was racing that it appeared as if the U.S. Ski Team was no longer supporting athletes in their abilities but now charging them based on what division they were a part of. For instance, the A-Team was not required to pay, but the skiers could actually earn money, while the B, C, and D-Teams were required to pay in order to make up for the overall team's expenses! Today, however, the organization has made a priority to support its athletes.

In response to the email, we wrote back, "Thank you for the nomination but Ryan Cochran-Siegle declines his nomination." We primarily declined because I didn't have the money to send him. Also, it was the first summer after high school, so I wanted Ryan to work and earn money to support his racing dreams.

It was actually interesting because when Ryan's scores were compared to the other skiers who were also born in 1992, he was ranked 4th in super G and 7th in giant slalom throughout the world. In the U.S., he ranked 1st in four out of five events, even coming in 6th in the Senior nationals Super G starting number 42. Since the U.S. Ski Team fully recognized his skills and his potential, they really wanted him to join them.

Today, the third generation Cochrans continue to make their mark in Alpine ski racing. In the early 2000s, there were four Cochrans on the U.S. Ski Team—Marilyn's son, Roger Brown; Bob's son, Jimmy; and two of Lindy's kids, Jessica and Timmy Kelley. Robby Kelley and my son, Ryan Cochran-Siegle rose up to follow in their steps and joined the U.S. Ski Team in 2011. Robby has retired and is now coaching and teaching while Ryan continues to race and won a silver medal at the Olympics in 2022 in Beijing, China.

Now there's a fourth generation of Cochran skiers! Most have learned or are learning to ski, although the youngest ones have not had the chance because they haven't started walking. There's a total of fifteen in this generation. Some have already started racing and dreaming of following in their cousins' footsteps, while others just ski for the love of the sport.

Whether or not they follow our legacy and make a name for themselves as elite ski racers, isn't important. What matters is having the opportunity to enjoy the outdoors in a sport like skiing!

CHAPTER 5

Cochran's Ski Area

First Beginnings

Today, I look back and see how well Dad and Mom taught all of us and passed on their hope for us to do the best that we could. They never pressured us to *be* the best, but encouraged us to *do* our best, and it truly led us to a life that we never could have imagined the first time we put on boots and skis.

In thinking about the history of Cochran's, it all started after Dad fulfilled his dream of putting up the rope-tow behind our house so we could train on weekday nights. Usually, we would get together with our friends from different ski clubs on Tuesday and Thursday nights. At the time, the news spread primarily through word-of-mouth and through ski parents talking to each other about their kids' activities. After all, we did not have any online social media in those days.

My parents never charged anyone an extravagant amount of money to use the ski area for recreation. As I recall, they first charged twenty-five cents to ride the original rope-tow for an afternoon. For the training on Tuesday and Thursday nights, people chipped in for gas for the rope-tow motor and took turns watching the safety gate to make sure nobody went through it. Dad and Mom could see how much fun it was for us so they would regularly coach all of the kids that showed up and other parents would be out there watching and waiting for their kids to ski down the hill.

In the early 60s, more property behind ours went up for sale, so Dad was able to purchase that as well, and that is where the current ski area is located. I started working at Cochran's whenever I could after I retired from my own ski racing. My sisters and brother also helped out whenever they could, although as their careers and families grew, they sometimes were busy moving about in the world.

Marilyn lived in Switzerland when her husband accepted a position with the university there. Roger was three years old when they left, and Douglas was born there. After five years, they moved back to the States. Marilyn and Roger both are now fluent in French.

Bob graduated from the University of Vermont Medical School and moved to Pennsylvania with his family for his residency in family medicine. After three years, they moved to New Hampshire where he joined the family practice in Walpole.

Lindy and her husband bought an old Vermont farmhouse in Starksboro, which they have renovated. When they bought it, it hadn't been lived in for thirty years, but had been used as a camp. There was no electricity. It had gas lights, a gas refrigerator, and a gas stove. They burned wood in a coal stove, which left a lot to be desired in heating the house!

After moving back from Washington, D.C., I worked at Cochran's more regularly on the weekends as a ski instructor. Depending on the school year and when the breaks were scheduled, I would also help out with the December and February ski vacation weeks that Dad and Mom would hold at Cochran's. I remember that Mom especially tried to run the programs for those vacation weeks.

When my sister Lindy's, daughter turned two, Lindy had taught her how to ski on her own. Other parents then asked Lindy to teach them how to teach their tot to ski. So, she started up an exciting new program called Ski Tots, where she taught the parents how to teach their tot. It was so much fun to see the little kids between the ages of three and five scattered all over the hill and learning to operate their own skis. We already had regular ski lessons for kids, which started at six years old and went up from there, which is what I taught.

Since Lindy was the inspiration behind the new program, she ran it for a time, focusing on instructing the participating parents on how to teach their little kids to ski. To this day, it's probably our most popular program and so much fun to watch. In fact, right now, my daughter is already beginning to teach her own two kids to ski, and there are other great-grandchildren who are picking up their own skills as well. It is amazing to stand back and watch how many little kids are skiing on their own at Cochran's. It is just as if you get to see the future of the sport unfold right in front of your very eyes on a daily basis!

Today's Operations

When my dad's health began to decline in the late 90s, interested families started to brainstorm how to keep Cochran's viable. The conclusion was to make Cochran's Ski Area a non-profit. It took some convincing with the government, but Cochran's was awarded a non-profit status in 1999. Now, Cochran's is operated by a Board of Directors, which started out with my mom, siblings, and other interested parents who wanted to keep Cochran's going. It also now includes some of our kids as well. The Board oversees staff evaluation and operations management, in addition to making sure that the daily focus of the ski area is to maintain the values and mission that my parents first put into action.

In addition to that, my nephew, Jimmy, who is Bob's son, runs the ski area year-round as the General Manager. He oversees the workstaff and the many volunteers who regularly help out by taking care of the lift and slopes, selling hot drinks, and other things like that. Besides Jimmy, there are two other people who are salaried—Carly, who manages the website and social media accounts, and Cory, who oversees mountain operations.

One of the things that we have always tried to do at Cochran's is to provide affordable skiing and boarding for anybody who wants to participate. We hear stories all the time about people who are looking to get involved without having to sacrifice an arm and a leg to do so. In response to that, we are happy to give out 10% of the passes we sell to families who need them.

For example, earlier this year, I was speaking with a woman who was originally from India and whose husband died during COVID. She was looking for something for her daughter to do during the winter. One of her neighbors recommended that she check out Cochran's, so both the mother and daughter went over there to take a look at everything. At that point, the woman called up Cochran's, spoke with Jimmy, and asked if she could get a discount for the season pass because of her situation.

After listening to her story, Jimmy told her, "We would be happy to *give* you a pass." Of course, the woman was extremely grateful, and her daughter was very happy, and they went on to enjoy the whole season together. That is just one of many examples to show how our mission to give back to the community works on a regular basis.

We also have some skiing programs that come with no charge, such as the Girls and Boys Club and the King Street Youth Program. With those programs, the kids come at no charge and use our public equipment while being taught by volunteer instructors that come and ski alongside them. The Girls and Boys Club also are provided a dinner so that the kids are able to return home after an adventurous afternoon with a full belly.

Besides the ski school, lessons are taught through after-school programs where about 800 kids sign up for an after-school program. Currently there are four towns involved: Williston, Richmond, Hinesburg, and Starksboro. Each town has a coordinator who is responsible for the sign-ups, instructors, and running the program.

Snow Motion is a program where all students in the district from K – 4th grade are taught to ski or snowboard. The kids are bussed to and from the ski area from their school during the school day for five weeks and spend an hour on the hill. If they don't have equipment, it is provided for them.

Kayla's Directory is another program for kids with disabilities that ski with a volunteer for an hour each Sunday. Cochran's Ski Club also offers race training and coaching to kids from age 6 through high school. On Friday nights, the public can ski for $5 from 3 p.m. to 8 p.m. and purchase a dinner special for $12.

As for the property, we own around 600 acres, with about 60 acres of that being leased to the ski area. Since a quarter of our budget depends on fundraising, we also have a yearly Rope-A-Thon where participants get people to sponsor them to make a donation to Cochran's. The activity is that each participant rides up the rope-tow as many times as they can during the Rope-A-Thon weekend during operating hours. It starts Friday at 4 and ends on Sunday at 4 when the area closes. The kids especially love it, since they are strong and agile enough to keep going up the rope, skiing down the slope, and repeating that cycle as many times as they want. Some of the younger nephews even claimed to do it a total of 500 times!

We get local businesses involved, such as the nearby restaurant that was happy to provide a free meal to each participant in the rotation. On weekends, we also offer free pancakes with fresh syrup from our very own maple trees for anyone who comes to join in. Jimmy put together a big grill on wheels for the event and flips the pancakes. Anyone who wants to donate for the cost of food is welcome to do so as well.

Speaking of pancakes and syrup, the maple syrup operation is a relatively new addition to the family operations, although a separate business from the ski area. It all started when we had a forester evaluate the property. He told us, "You know, you have a lot of maple trees on this land. You could have a really nice operation here."

From there, four of the nephews got together—Marilyn's sons, Roger and Douglas; Bob's son, Jimmy; and Lindy's son, Timmy—and began looking into the maple syrup business. They built their own sugarhouse, put in around 5,000 taps, and then Timmy came up with the unique name—Slopeside Syrup! Today, they operate with 20,000+ taps and have evolved to include two businesses: Slopeside Syrup and Untapped. Roger and Douglas teamed up with Ted King, a professional bicyclist, and Andrew Gardner, a former Nordic skiing coach to develop Untapped, which distributes maple syrup as an energy source. Jimmy and Timmy run Slopeside Syrup, which collects the sap from the maple trees and turns it into syrup.

As our family continues to grow and Cochran's Ski Area also expands, I regularly continue to look back, forward, and all around me at what is taking place. As I look back to how we started and where I came from, I am thankful for the strong foundation that my parents put in place for all of us. As I look around at where my siblings, our children, and grandchildren are at and all the people that we have brought together to be a part of our family's operations, I am excited to see how much we have been able to give back to the community. As I look forward to the future, I am hopeful about how things will continue to develop. Most of all, I expect that we will keep building upon the strong foundation that was given to us by Mom and Dad and preserve it with great dedication for years to come.

Among all the wonderful accolades we have received, one of the most beautiful sentiments was from a dad whose children learned to ski at Cochran's. He remarked to us that when he would drive up the hill to the upper parking lot, watching the ski area unfold before him, it was a moment that consistently would take his breath away. His mind would lovingly refer to that as: "Ahh! Prozac Mountain!"

Governor Howard Dean, former governor of Vermont, brought his kids to learn to ski there. He called Cochran's "an Vermont State Treasure." Often people refer to Cochran's as "magical."

Part Two

CHAPTER 6

The Cochran Way

Reflecting on Winning Gold

After the Olympics, I began to think deeply about what it was that allowed me to win. *Was it skill?* I asked myself. *Was it luck?* While I recognized that both of those factors played a part of it, there was something more that allowed me to ski faster on those two particular runs, on that exact day, and under those conditions. I realized that the additional factor was that I had the mental edge to win because of the way that I had been trained for so many years.

In thinking back over the lessons that Dad gave me and my sisters and brother so many years ago, I am greatly appreciative of the "Cochran Way" that was taught to all of us. In turn, we have been able to pass it down to our own children and I have been able to teach it to many young people who come to me for instruction.

Taking one specific lesson as an example, I can see how Dad's emphasis on learning the course greatly benefited me more than I can say for my modern counterparts. Today, the whole system is set up differently and athletes do not even have time to memorize or visualize the whole course.

In fact, coaches will say, "You don't have to hike the whole course, just memorize the tough spots!"

Instead, my dad saw it differently. When he first put up the ski area with its rope-tow and 14 gates behind our house when we were young, he noticed something important. The hill was not very big at all, only about 14 to 16 seconds long, but he recognized that when we and our friends trained, it was not until the third or fourth practice run that our skiing time suddenly improved.

At that point, Dad started to think, *What's going on? Why all of a sudden on that third or fourth run are they going so much faster?* He finally recognized that it was not until that point that we felt comfortable enough with the course because we had gotten to know it and began to expect what lay ahead.

From that moment, he started to train us to hike the course and think ahead. "In a race," Dad told us, "you won't be able to run the course 1, 2, or 3 times to really get to know it. That's why if you memorize it and visualize yourself running it before you get there, then it will be easier for you."

I really believe that Dad was onto something critical. I think that athletes gain a lot by visualizing running the entire course and developing that skill over time. Every time a skier visualizes running the whole course, they will create a pathway through their brain and their reaction time will be that much quicker when they actually go through the run.

Another thing that both Dad and Mom always taught us is that we were capable of winning. This especially helped me in my Olympic race. Leading up to that day, I fully believed that I was able to win. I didn't know if I would, but there was no doubt in my mind that I was as good as anyone else on that hill.

Beginning in the spring of 1971, everyone knew that the next year was an Olympic year and that the Winter Games would be held in Sapporo, Japan. The media, our extended family, my friends, and our fans believed that there was a good chance that all four of us Cochran kids would end up as part of the U.S. Ski Team. We were, after all, "The Skiing Cochrans: America's First Family of Skiing," or so the press called us.

All throughout that spring, summer, and fall, after Marilyn, Bobby, and I were named to the A-Team, I was asked over and over again, "How do you think the team will do in the Olympics?"

My answer was consistent: "We are capable of winning. We have lots of talented skiers and we could win."

The press didn't have as much confidence in the rest of the team as I did, so their next question was always, "Well, let's be realistic. What do you think *your* chances are?"

Once again, I would answer, "I don't know what will happen at the Olympics, but I do know that I am as capable as anyone else. I've worked hard and I've developed the skills I need to win. I don't know if I *will* win, but I know that I *can* win!"

As the season progressed, I used all of the lessons that Dad and Mom taught me. As it turned out, because I was asked over and over again how I thought I would do and consistently gave the answer that "I don't know if I *will* win, but I know that I *can* win," I was repeating an affirmation, even though I had never heard of that term at the time. Since then, I have learned how powerful an affirmation can be to set up expectations in your brain so that whatever you expect to happen is exactly what *will* happen!

By the time I got to the Olympics, I believed in the deepest part of my soul that I was capable of winning. I also knew that I wanted to win and that I deserved to win. That was my mental edge. In all honesty, my sister, my brother, and other competitors on the course were just as capable of winning as I was, and some of them may have had even more skills than I did! I believe that the reason that I won was because I had the mental edge based on all of the things that I was brought up to believe about who I was and what I could do.

My Own Coaching Style

After my big win and retirement from the U.S. Ski Team, I began to give more thought to how I practiced and began to develop my own training style. I have also thought a lot more about the "Cochran Way" and how it has helped me in my life. I eventually put together a training workbook for athletes to help them focus on their own perspective as they head to the slopes for practice every day.

When it all comes down to it, I find that stories are extremely powerful in coaching athletes in today's world. I tell stories about my dad's World War II experiences. I tell stories about my childhood, including how I was known as "the pokey little puppy" of the family as I grew up, which accidentally led me to being left behind by my family at the beach one day. I tell stories about skiing, like how I did not like downhill races very much because I did not know what to do. Stories draw each athlete in and help me connect with them when we first meet.

After that, one of the things I like to do is understand the particular mindset of each individual athlete. Some years ago, I read a book called *Mindset* by Carol Dweck, a psychologist who explained that there are two different kinds of mindsets—the fixed mindset and the growth mindset. With the fixed mindset, an individual is defined by their results whereas, with the growth mindset, the individual is focused on the process.

To reach that conclusion, Dweck created an experiment with 10-year-old boys in a school setting to study how they would react to certain projects and be able to evaluate what that meant about thought processes. In the experiment, she first gave them a problem that she knew they could all solve and watched them react by individually demonstrating their belief that they were very smart. She also responded by telling them, "You know, you guys are so smart. I knew you would be able to do this!"

The second time around, she wanted to see what their reaction would be if she gave them a problem that she knew would be too hard for them to solve. Once she passed it out, the majority of the boys in the room shut down. The boys felt that if they had a problem that they couldn't solve, and they were supposed to be the smartest kids in the class, instead of attempting to solve it, it would be better for them to not even try.

There was one little boy, however, who reacted completely differently. Instead of shutting down, he smiled at the psychologist and seemed very excited to receive the hard problem. He said, "I thought you were just going to give us easy problems the whole time to solve!" Now that he had a problem that he really had to think about, it didn't matter to him if the first way he thought about it didn't work. He would continue to try and think about the challenge differently until he eventually figured it out!

The psychologist realized from that experiment that most people have a fixed mind that is set on results, whereas very few people have a mind that is focused on the challenge of the thinking process instead.

In the same way, I try to get athletes to focus on the process more than on the result. Most athletes are more worried about the results—they want to win a race, they want to beat their competitors, they don't want other competitors to beat them, they're trying to qualify for a certain team, and so on. With that fixed mindset, they are unable to get out there and truly perform at their best, so I work with them to change their thoughts to a growth mindset.

In my coaching workbook, I particularly emphasize this whole shift in one place that talks about pressure-producing thoughts, which are the fixed-mindset thoughts, and pressure-reducing thoughts, which are the growth-mindset thoughts. Another thing that helps is going through a session on emotions, which talks specifically about how the feelings of athletes impact their performance, what kind of inner climate that creates, and how they can compare their emotions to certain energies that either help or hurt their performance.

I also like to draw in examples of individuals where different emotions have affected them in either a pleasant or unpleasant way. If it is unpleasant—such as nervousness, fear, anxiety, frustration, or anger, then it might result in them shutting down. I know that other coaches sometimes try and get their athletes angry because it sometimes motivates them to do better, but I often use the example of tennis player John McEnroe to make a point. John McEnroe was a phenomenal athlete who harbored a lot of anger and even ranked first in the world during part of his career. In that sense, his anger did not stop him from getting really good results, but it did add to his tension. I feel that if John McEnroe had been able to play with a pure love of the game, then he truly would have been unstoppable!

I also use the example of Mikaela Shiffrin to talk about what happens when emotions leave you unable to perform at a level of which you are capable. Mikaela first competed on the World Cup when she was sixteen years old in two events—giant slalom and slalom. In her second year, by American standards, she did well in giant slalom, often finishing in the top fifteen. But she truly shined in slalom, winning five slaloms and finishing in the top ten in four more. She was phenomenal! She dominated World Cup slaloms the next year, winning five and the Olympic gold.

The next year, she decided that she wanted to win the overall title and knew that she could not earn enough points just from slalom to be the overall champion so she set a goal to improve her giant slalom. When she tied for first in the opening giant slalom in Soelden, Austria, her strategy seemed like it would work. However, when she went to the first slalom race of the season in Finland, she did not do so well, which was unlike her. Even though Mikaela finished 11th in one race, then 5th in the next race, and then 4th in the race after that, it was not like her because she was capable of so much more. People began to wonder, *What's going on with her? Why isn't she dominating like she did last year?*

There was even an article in a ski racing magazine that I remember reading where she was quoted saying something significant about the time that she finally began to make a comeback. Mikaela said that she finally remembered that slalom was fun for her. My gut tells me that when she was racing and focusing on how to improve in giant slalom, she was not operating at a high energy, positive emotions level. Instead, she was struggling because, when it was not fun for her anymore, she started to feel those negative emotions coming in that quickly depleted her energy.

As I think back over everything that I have learned and seen throughout the years, I recognize that most of what I now know about sports psychology, I did not know when I was racing. Yet, since I have been in that position and remember what it was like, I am able to take in a lot of material and formulate my own thoughts and information about it.

Back in the '90s, for example, the Vermont Principal's Association, which was the governing body for high school sports, asked me to be a keynote speaker for a leadership conference for high school girls. I said, "Sure, I'd love to do that!" Then I began to put my thoughts together.

Around the same time, I was reading an amazing book called *Mental Toughness Training for Sports* by James Loehr where I learned about how emotions affect your performance. He presented it a little differently than I do. He made a graph about emotions with the positive energy levels on the left side and the negative on the right side, which is opposite to how a math graph is written. I created the graph with the positive energy levels on the right, to keep it compatible with math.

At that point, I began to realize how my study of sports psychology was simply a pattern of reading and experimenting, and then thinking about my family and our experiences growing up to recognize how everything went together. The more I read about mindset, the more I perfectly understood key things about how my family worked together.

For instance, my older sister is a perfectionist and was only 11 months when I came along, and almost 2 years old when Bobby was born after me. She basically started being Mom's little helper as soon as she could walk.

When we were growing up, Mom would turn to Marilyn and ask her to do something. For instance, at dinner one summer night, Mom asked Marilyn to get the ice cream out of the freezer, but Marilyn immediately turned to me and said, "No, Barbara Ann, you go do it." This happened very often as we continued to grow up.

I did not know that I could refuse to do something that my sister commanded me to do, so I always operated that way from the time I was a little girl who constantly followed my big sister around. If Mom told Marilyn to do something, then I fully expected for that specific task to soon be turned over to me so that I had to do it.

It was not until I was 13 years old that I learned that I did not have to listen to my older sister. We had a cousin over at our house who was going to UVM and had been kicked out the last two weeks of school for throwing a chair on a bonfire in the fraternity driveway. He was not able to stay on campus and could not take classes, so he got in touch with Mom and Dad and asked if he could come over and stay with us.

While he was there, Mom asked Marilyn to get the ice cream out of the freezer, which was on the porch since we were not able to get the freezer downstairs into the basement. Marilyn responded, "No! Barbara Ann, you go do it!" I was sitting right next to Bubby and got up to go do it, but Bubby immediately put his hand on my shoulder and pushed me back down into my chair.

"No, Barbara Ann," he said, "you sit down. Marilyn, *you* go get the ice cream."

I had been so trained to just do what Marilyn told me over the years that it was not until that exact moment when I finally understood that it was perfectly fine for me to refuse to listen to my sister!

As I have developed my own understanding of the important life lessons that are helpful for athletes, I have combined many of my thoughts into a workbook for athletes called "How to Gain the Competitive Edge." Another set of materials that is helpful for my trainees is a blog post that is based off a mindset workshop that I did on Zoom during COVID for a camp in Sugarloaf, Maine. In both cases, I make sure to customize my training to fit the individual, whether it is a single hour-long session or a package of five or ten coaching sessions spread out over the course of several months.

Most of all, I find it very rewarding to work with athletes because I am passionate about skiing, keeping our mindset in the right place, and sports in any form. As I think back to my dad's dreams for us as a family and then look forward to the future, I am hopeful about the future of athletics. I expect to keep on pointing many more young people who are growing up within a particular area of sports by encouraging them to do the very best that they can do.

CHAPTER 7

The Competitive Edge

The Mental Preparation Factor

In 1972, I won a gold medal at the winter Olympics in Sapporo, Japan. I've often wondered why I won. My sister, Marilyn, and brother, Bob, were there as well and had just as much talent as I did. Why didn't they win?

The French dominated ski racing that whole year up until the Olympics. Why didn't they continue to win?

A Spaniard, Francisco Fernandez Ochoa, who had never won a World Cup race prior to the Games, won the men's slalom. Why was he able to win?

At Wimbledon one year, a player who ranked 114th nearly upset top-seeded Ivan Lendl before losing in the fifth set 6 – 1. How could he play so well in four sets and then fall apart in the fifth?

In Game One of the World Series in 1988, the Los Angeles Dodgers were behind runs 4 – 3 at the bottom of the ninth. Kirk Gibson was at bat. There were two outs with one man on base. The count was three balls, two strikes. This was a tight situation and made even tighter by the fact that Kirk Gibson couldn't run because of his bad knees. Yet, he went on to hit a home run. Under those circumstances, how could he perform?

At the Superbowl in 1989, the San Francisco 49'ers were losing to Cincinnati by 16 – 13 with little more than three minutes to play. The ball was back on their own three-yard line. Yet, Joe Montana, the quarterback for the 49'ers, was able to move the ball up-field and score a touchdown before the time ran out. San Francisco won the game 20 – 16. How did that happen?

In 1992, Dan O'Brien was a sure bet to win the Olympic Decathlon but failed to make the U.S. Olympic team. Just four years later in 1996, not only did he make the team, but he also won the gold medal. What brought that turnaround?

Dan Jansen competed in four Olympics—Sarajevo in 1984, Calgary in 1988, Albertville in 1992, and Lillehammer in 1994. In the last three Games, he was considered to be the best 500-meter speed skater in the world. Yet, in all those races, he failed to win a medal. His gold came in his very last Olympic race of his whole career—the 1,000-meters. How do you explain that?

In 1996, at the Masters, Greg Norman went into the last day leading by six strokes. It was an insurmountable lead. He played brilliantly the whole season, yet on the very last day, he failed miserably, not only losing his lead but also the championship. What brought on that disaster?

After 86 years of coming up short in their attempts to win the World Series, the Boston Red Sox had dug themselves into a hole in the American League Championship playoffs. They lost three games straight to the New York Yankees. They had to win the next four games to be able to play in the World Series. No team in the history of baseball had ever lost the first three games and come back to win the next four! Not only did they accomplish that great feat by winning the next four, but they also won four straight games in the World Series to be crowned World Champions in 2004, effectively ending their 86-year drought. How can that sudden success be explained?

At the Superbowl in 2017, the Atlanta Falcons had built a lead of 28 – 3 over the Boston Patriots by the third quarter. Being

Boston fans, I remember some of my family members saying, "The Patriots are done! No way can they come back from this deficit!" Yet, within the last seconds of the fourth quarter, they tied the game to go into overtime. It was an exciting game with the Patriots pulling out the win in overtime. How was that possible?

The list of examples continues on throughout sports history, but the question remains: What made the difference? Why can some athletes rise above what is expected of them and win great titles, while others who appear to dominate a sport suddenly fail to perform at their best in the championships? At the same time, why are other competitors able to reach the top and stay there, no matter what the contest?

Although there are many factors that contribute to the outcome, the most important is mental preparation. At the Olympics in 1972, I prepared better mentally than I had for any other race.

Francisco Fernandez Ochoa said that when he woke up that morning for the World Cup race, he knew that he was going to win. There was no doubt or apprehension in his mind.

Nicholas Pereira, the eighteen-year-old tennis player who nearly upset Ivan Lendl at Wimbledon told himself after the fourth set, *I'm not going to get excited about winning the 4th set. Now is when I have to beat him. Now is when I have to start playing.* It was those thoughts that led to his defeat in the fifth set.

Kirk Gibson had nothing to lose by just trying to meet the ball. He was out there to do his best. It was the only way he could contribute to the team on the field.

Joe Montana was thrilled with the situation in the Superbowl. He later told reporters, "You want this type of game, with your back against the wall and the score really tight. My teammates showed they are true athletes today when the pressure is on. That's the way you want to win the game."

Dan O'Brien felt tremendous pressure in 1992 to win a gold medal. As a result, he fell apart. In 1996, he was able to mentally handle it better, make the Olympic team, and win gold.

Dan Jansen had to overcome enormous emotional difficulties when his sister died on the very same day that he was competing in the 500-meters in Calgary. Although he didn't realize it at the time, he was tortured with feelings of betrayal and a belief that if his sister was dying, he should be there with her, not competing in the Olympics.

Greg Norman admitted that he choked in the Masters.

Watching the big turnaround for the Boston Red Sox was a lot of fun, not only because I'm a die-hard Red Sox fan, but because the players were having such a good time themselves. They truly demonstrated how much they loved to play baseball and how much they cared for each other as a team.

The quarterback for the Patriots, Tom Brady, believed anything was possible and kept encouraging his team to go out, execute, and play. With that belief in his team and the constant positive encouragement, the team scored a touchdown in overtime to win 34 – 28.

Skill or Mental Preparation?

What determines the outcome of any competition, whether it be a game, a race, a meet, or a match? Is it mastery of skill? Is it luck? Emotions? Thoughts? Destiny? If you had to decide what percentage of the result is dependent on skill and what percentage of the result is dependent on mental preparation, how would you mark it down?

SKILL: ____ %
MENTAL PREPARATION: ____ %

(Let me give you a hint: The percentages should add up to 100!)

This leads to another question. Which comes first? Does an athlete perform well because he's mastered the skills necessary to win? Or does he win because he has created an inner climate to access the same exact skills that are necessary to win?

Many athletes—and parents and coaches, for that matter—assume that the final result of any competition is because the athlete, or team, demonstrated better skills in the competition. Therefore, they would say that the most important factor in determining the outcome of any contest is how skilled the athlete or team really is. However, that would greatly underestimate the power of mental preparation.

At any level of sport, whether you are a beginner or a world-class athlete, I believe that the final outcome depends far more on the mental skills that you have mastered than the technical skills that you have learned in your sport. To go back to our diagram from earlier, I would fill it out like this:

SKILL: 10 % (or less!)
MENTAL PREPARATION: 90 % (or more!)

Of course, this is *not* to say that if you're a little league pitcher, you could do well in the major leagues just because you have mastered the mental skills necessary to perform well. What it *does* mean, however, is that with mental preparation, you would do well within your level against other little league teams.

Whenever you compete in a sport, you compete against others that have roughly the same skill level as you do within a certain range. If you're playing J.V. soccer in high school, you'll be playing against others that are around your age and have about the same experience. Granted, some players may have dedicated their young lives to the sport of soccer and therefore have gained more experience and skill than the average player. But, with a few exceptions, you will have roughly the same skills as others you are competing against. In that sense, it is not so much the difference in technical skill that makes the difference, but it is about how well you can create an inner climate through positive mental preparation to access the skills that you have already developed.

When you look at teams or individual athletes who have dominated their sport over time, you realize that, yes, they have talent. Yet, it is not the talent that puts them over the top consistently. It is because they have prepared mentally.

"Teams do not go physically flat; they go mentally stale."
Vince Lombardi, former football coach of the Green Bay Packers

---

What Exactly Is Mental Preparation?

Are there contests in which the most skilled athlete did *not* overcome all the other lesser skilled athletes? Of course! What is the difference? Mental preparation, or all of those things that go on between the ears during a competition including one's goals, thoughts, attitude, and beliefs, and then, ultimately, what the body experiences emotionally.

Athletes must learn to focus their energy and perform at peak levels to become the best of the best, or simply to *do* their best. The success of a competition is as much determined by the mental readiness of the athlete as the skill level that he has already attained. The best trained athlete can fall flat on his face if he is not prepared mentally.

When I competed in the Olympics, I was twenty-one years old. I had been racing since the age of five. I had been a member of the U.S. Ski Team for six years. It was my fourth year of racing abroad and my very first time in Japan. Yet, for this race, I prepared better mentally than I had for any other race. Some of that was accidental, but some of that was part of my routine.

Here is a look into my own process and what I did to succeed: **Became mentally tough**: I loved competition. Even when I didn't think that I had a chance of winning, I wanted to compete against the best. I liked to watch them and to see what they were doing that I was not. Often, my performance improved when I skied with better racers. I also could judge how much more I had to improve to get to that higher level.

Set goals: As a youngster, I had set a goal that I wanted to win a gold medal in the Olympics. I did not obsess about it, but that thought was always there like a planted seed—just waiting for the right conditions and waiting to be nurtured, to grow, and to blossom.

The goal that I focused on overall was to do my best. That did not mean to *be* the best, just to *do* my best. If I skied faster than any other racer and that was my best, so much the better. But I also had to accept the times that I had performed to the best of my ability and lost, which occurred far more often! For example, in 1972, the same year that I won the gold medal at the Olympics, I actually only won two total races—the slalom at the Olympics and the Sugar Slalom at Stowe, Vermont, which was a long-standing, fun race in the spring where racers were treated to sugar-on-snow.

Reduced pressure: I only allowed myself to think thoughts that reduced pressure. I told myself, *Just do the best you can. Work on your skills and let the results take care of themselves. If the French can win, I can win, too!*

At the Olympics, after I was leading after the first run, I did start to get nervous. I started to think, *What would it be like if I did win? What if I did win?* But I realized that I had to calm down or I was not going to be able to do anything. So, I told myself, *Okay, you've won the first run and not very many people have done that! No matter how this race turns out, you can always be proud of your first run.*

I thought about my dad and what he had told me two years before the Olympics at my competition in the World Championships. After the first run, I was in 6th place. I wanted to move up and win a medal. Dad was standing at the top of the course before the second run. I was nervously waiting for the start. I confided in Dad and told him that I was worried about how I was going to do. He responded, "I always thought you were 'the cool cucumber' in the family!" And I thought about that and agreed, "Yeah, I guess I am!" Then I stopped worrying and continued with the race to win the silver medal. At the Olympics, I thought about that same conversation, and it calmed me down.

My last comment to myself was, *You should do all right!*

Chose a positive attitude: The subconscious mind believes anything you tell it. So, I just told it, *You can do this! Maybe not as well as you'd like, or as well as someone else, but you can do this!* With practice, I knew that I would get better.

In training, I didn't worry about the 59 turns that were bad. Instead, I thought about the one turn that I did well. I knew that if I did one turn well, I could do more.

I concentrated on my skills, not my results. I could control what I was doing, but I had no control over what anyone else was doing.

I also gave myself the freedom not to win. No matter how the race turned out, as long as I had tried to do my best, I knew that I was a good person. I was okay!

Believed in myself: I believed that if I worked hard enough, anything was possible. In Sapporo, I knew that I had developed the skills to win the slalom and the giant slalom.

I also believed that the most important thing was striving to reach my goals. I learned tremendous lessons through the whole attempt, rather than just through the actual attainment. The gold medal was the icing on the cake!

Practiced affirmations: An affirmation is a positive declaration stated in the present, as if the desired result is already happening. I reinforced the beliefs that I already had with similar thoughts and overcame any undesirable beliefs with new ideas.

When I was 21, I had no idea what an affirmation was. It wasn't until many years later that I became aware of them. In looking back, I realize now that I had already practiced affirmations before the Olympics simply because I answered the same questions over and over. Reporters from newspapers, magazines, and television wanted to know how the U.S. Ski Team would do in the Olympics. They also wanted to know what my chances were in winning a gold medal.

My response was always the same: "The U.S. has a very good chance of winning medals. There is a lot of talent on the team. Both the men and the women are capable of winning." As far as I was concerned, I told them, "I know I have the skills to win. I don't know if that will happen on that particular day, but yes, I am capable of winning."

Visualized myself doing well: In every competition, I ran the courses in my head before I ever left the starting gate. I knew where the gates were, where the bumps were, where the ice was, what line I wanted to be on, where I should start my turn, and where I could step to gain more speed. I saw myself completing the course and completing it to the best of my ability.

Controlled my emotions: All of the seven things listed above led to this next part where I was able to create an inner climate that was calm, confident, focused, and truly loving what I was doing. Because my emotions were under control, I could do my best. And I already knew that my best was good enough!

Before going to the Olympics, I didn't know if I would win but I knew that I could win in both the slalom and the giant slalom. I won the gold in the slalom and came in eleventh in the giant slalom. I believe that my gold medal performance was directly related to my mental preparedness.

With positive mental preparation, you can learn how to become your own best friend in performance situations. Some aspects of this whole process include:

1. Choosing thoughts that lead to improved performance,
2. Controlling performance anxiety,
3. Understanding what causes "choking" and taking steps to prevent it,
4. Recognizing the beliefs that enhance or hinder performance,
5. Understanding how the subconscious mind can sabotage even outstanding efforts,
6. Using visualization to achieve desired results,
7. Cultivating mental toughness,
8. Developing the characteristics of a top athlete,
9. and much more . . .

How to Gain the Competitive Edge

Over the years, as I have been asked to speak to various teams and groups about what being a gold medalist was like and what it took to become one, I developed my own ideas into a program called "How to Gain the Competitive Edge." Athletes soon began working with me to improve their performance and I talked to teams about having the mental preparation to win. As my sport program evolved, I also taught coaches and parents of aspiring athletes how to understand and support their own athletes.

In the following chapters, I will explain my ideas further on "How to Gain the Competitive Edge" based on nine factors of mental preparation and how each one impacts performance. The program teaches you to:

- Understand what it takes to be mentally tough and how to choose mental toughness
- Evaluate your attitude and how it affects your results, including what works and what doesn't
- Discover your own beliefs and how they are related to your performance
- Increase your success by destroying limits and expanding dreams through goal-setting
- Understand how emotions affect your performance and how to control them
- Focus your thoughts before, during, and after a competition
- Break down blocks with different modalities
- Change behaviors and beliefs that limit you by using affirmations
- Use visualization to create your image of success

We have an exciting adventure ahead, so let's get started!

CHAPTER 8

Mental Toughness

What is Mental Toughness?

Have you ever felt that, when it comes to competition, you are your own worst enemy? Why? What does that mean? More than likely, it means that you are frustrated because, no matter what you do, you cannot come close to performing your best—to achieving close to your potential.

You may train well. You may be able to perform well when you're not competing. You may even be able to execute amazing skills when you're horsing around. But get you into a game and have you leave the start in an actual race? That's a whole different story.

If you feel anything like this, as if you are out of luck because you just weren't born with the right genes for mental toughness, do not despair! Very few athletes have a natural ability to maintain composure during competition. Some struggle with the skill more than others.

The good news is that mental toughness is just like any other skill—it can be learned! With practice, the skills that involve mental toughness can be improved. Everyone can learn how to create an inner climate that controls their fears and emotions and is fully conducive to performing well.

I love Yogi Berra's wisdom concerning baseball on this matter:

> *"Baseball is 90% mental—the other half is physical."*
> Yogi Berra, former baseball player and coach

There are two emotions that affect mental toughness more than any others—love and fear. Mental toughness becomes much easier to develop when an athlete loves what she is doing no matter where she is—in practice, in competition, with teammates, under coaches, alongside friends, with family, and regardless of the weather and other conditions.

But fear? This is where being mentally tough really comes into play. In my work with athletes, they've shared a whole variety of fears—fear of not being good enough, fear of disappointing the many people around them, fear of making mistakes, fear of being criticized, fear of losing or failing, fear of making a fool of themselves, fear of choking, fear of not living up to their own expectations or those of others, fear of losing a skill that they have already learned, fear of getting hurt, fear of being in the limelight, fear of succeeding, fear of winning, and fear of the people who are watching. The list goes on and on!

Being mentally tough means handling all of those fears and maintaining composure in the midst of it. The skills that go along with developing mental toughness include:

1. becoming aware of yourself—your attitude, beliefs, emotions, and thoughts;
2. choosing thoughts that improve your emotions and create a positive attitude;
3. destroying blocks to overcome barriers that are holding you back;

4. developing affirmations and visualizations to produce the results you really want; and
5. taking action.

"Toughness is in the soul and spirit, not in muscles."
Alex Karras, former pro-football player and actor

Characteristics of Top Athletes

Successful athletes have a number of similar traits in how they approach the game. According to James Loehr, a sports psychologist and the author of *Mental Toughness Training for Sports*, there are nine characteristics that make up mental strength. Top athletes are:

- Self-motivated and self-directed. Top athletes compete in their sport because *they* want to. They love what they are doing, and they live for their sport. No one has to tell them to train. They know what they have to do to be the best. They are driven internally.
- Positive but realistic. Athletes with mental strength focus on the positives and on what is possible. They look at the glass as half-full. They refuse to complain or criticize. They are optimistic, yet realistic.
- In control of emotions. No matter what happens, top athletes control their emotions. They never allow anger, frustration, or fear to dominate their actions.
- Calm and relaxed under fire. Top athletes get charged up in tough situations. They love the challenge and the

pressure. They see each difficult opportunity as a chance to shine, rather than something that will defeat them.
- Highly energetic and ready for action. No matter how bad the situation might be, top athletes can pump themselves up and compete to the best of their ability.
- Determined. No matter what others might say or feel about them, athletes with mental strength know that they will succeed. They will do whatever it takes to reach their goals.
- Mentally alert and focused. Top athletes concentrate on the skills that they need to perform. They focus on the task at hand and live in the moment. They tune in to what is really important and tune out the rest.
- Doggedly self-confident. Mentally strong athletes believe in themselves. They know that they have the skills to do well. They are not intimidated by their competitors.
- Fully responsible. Top athletes hold themselves accountable for their actions. They never use excuses or blame others for their failures. They know that their success is fully their responsibility.

Here is an exercise to help you get started and see where your mental toughness lies! Using the chart on the following page, identify your strengths and weaknesses of mental preparation. Be honest! The chart is simply a tool to help you reflect on your personal characteristics. There is nothing good or bad about where you fit in. It simply is a means to understand where you are at and where you can improve.

How to Gain the Competitive Edge Worksheet

Characteristics of Mental Strength

Using the chart below, identify your strengths and weaknesses of mental preparation by placing a check in the appropriate column:

CHARACTERISTICS:	Never	Sometimes	Always
(1) Self-Motivated & Self-Directed			
I do it because I want to. No one has to tell me to do it. I love what I'm doing. I do it because I enjoy it!			
(2) Positive but Realistic			
I don't complain, criticize, or find fault with other teammates, my coach, the referees, timers, fans, weather, conditions, etc.; I build rather than destroy. I focus on success, on what can happen, and on what is possible. I am both optimistic and realistic.			
(3) In Control of Emotions			
No matter what the conditions (bad refereeing, stupid mistakes, obnoxious opponents, poor conditions, etc.), I control my anger, frustration, and fear—or any other negative emotion.			
(4) Calm & Relaxed Under Fire			

HIKE THE COURSE

CHARACTERISTICS:	Never	Sometimes	Always
I love pressure! I love tough situations. I perform best when the odds are against me. When the pressure is on, I see it as a challenge, an opportunity to explore the outer limits of my potential.			
(5) Highly Energetic & Ready for Action			
No matter how I feel or how bad the situation might be, I can pump myself up and energize myself to compete to the best of my ability.			
(6) Determined			
I am relentless in pursuit of my goals. I don't care if others don't understand my determination. I will do whatever I need to do to reach my goals.			
(7) Mentally Alert & Focused			
I tune in to what is important and tune out what is not. I focus on what is at hand. I concentrate on the skills I need to perform.			
(8) Doggedly Self-Confident			
I am confident. I believe in myself. I know I have the ability to perform well. I am not intimidated by my competitors.			
(9) Fully Responsible			
I take full responsibility for my actions. I do not use excuses. I either did it or didn't do it. My destiny as an athlete is in my hands.			

Material adapted from Mental Toughness Training for Sports by James E. Loehr. Chart developed by Barbara Ann Cochran for Barbara Ann Cochran Coaching, a business to teach people how to improve performance through mental preparation. For more information, go to www.sportssuccesscoaching.com.

A concept concerning mental toughness that deserves more explanation is accepting the challenge of a better competitor. This is an important factor in becoming doggedly self-confident, as seen in #8 from the above chart.

Accepting the Challenge of a Better Competitor

Our growth comes when we challenge ourselves and stretch ourselves to our limits. We experience improvement when we compete against the best athletes who are all around us. Rather than hoping that the best competitor won't show up for an event, we gain more from competing against that particular competitor. There are two reasons for this:

- The first reason is that we often perform better when we play against someone who is better than we are. We see their skills and begin to subconsciously imitate them or, at the very least, we see what it takes to do the skill at a higher level.
- The second reason for accepting the challenge of a better competitor is that we now have a gauge to measure how far we have to go to reach that next level.

To use an example that I have mentioned before, let's think about playing tennis. I'm an okay tennis player—not great, mind you, but okay. I've never competed in any tournaments, but I definitely enjoy playing against friends and family. Although I usually lose, I do have fun.

Sometimes, I watch a major tournament on TV—either Wimbledon or the U.S. Open. When I play tennis right after I watch the professionals play, my skills improve quite noticeably. I don't think about what I'm doing, but because I observed what the best players in the world did, my brain is subconsciously able to pick up the skills that they were executing. My body adjusted and allowed me to improve my game.

I have often witnessed this on the field many times. As I've watched a team sport like soccer, field hockey, baseball, or football, I've noticed that a team often plays better when they're competing against a team that has more experience and can execute the skills better than they can. On the other hand, when the same team comes up against a less skilled or less experienced team, their own play deteriorates.

One year, when I was coaching track and field at the high school where I was teaching, my best long-distance runner came up to me. She was excited because she found out some news about who was participating in our first meet against one of the toughest schools in the state, MMU. Their best long-distance runner happened to also be the best in the state. Ann was thrilled when she learned that her competitor was on a class trip to Europe and would not be competing in the upcoming meet. She was delighted because she thought it meant that she had a good chance to win.

I am sure my reaction surprised her. I told Ann that she should be disappointed that she didn't have the opportunity to race against the best long-distance runner in the state! I pointed out, "Sure, you have a great chance to win. But what would it mean for you without the best competitor being there?"

The other possibility was that Ann could have competed well against the best long-distance runner and won. What would that victory mean? Wouldn't that mean more to Ann than winning without the greatest competitor being there?

On the other hand, let's say that the MMU athlete did beat Ann. What were the possibilities for Ann to do better because she was competing against someone whom she saw as more skilled? Even if she came in second, she could have had a personal best because she competed against a skilled athlete.

I felt that the opportunity for Ann to achieve her best was better if she was able to compete against the best long-distance runner in the state. I felt that coming in second was more valuable than winning without her there. If she did win *with* her there, that would be the most meaningful of all.

CHAPTER 9

Attitude

Attitude Determines Everything

Lou Holtz, one of the most successful NCAA football coaches in collegiate history explained the differences between ability, motivation, and attitude: "Ability is what you're capable of doing. Motivation determines what you do. Attitude determines how well you do it."

James Loehr, a sports psychologist, and author of *Mental Toughness Training for Sports*, described attitudes as "nothing more than habits of thought" and further explained, "Attitudes are the 'stuff' of which champions are made."

Carol Dweck, a Stanford University psychologist who studied achievement and success, discovered that there are two ways to think about one's own abilities and traits. Some people believe that their basic qualities like athletic ability or intelligence are set, which she calls a "fixed mindset." People with a fixed mindset spend their time documenting their traits rather than developing them because they believe that it is the talented people that create success.

Dweck also found that some people think differently. They believe that their athletic ability or intelligence or creativity can be developed with hard work. They trust that they can improve as long as they are dedicated to improving. Indeed, according to *Mindset Works*, "Research shows that people with a growth mindset reach higher levels of success than people with fixed mindset beliefs."

The WordNet dictionary defines attitude as "a complex mental state involving beliefs and feelings and values and dispositions to act in certain ways."

For an athlete, attitude is everything. Attitude determines how you look at different situations. Attitude determines how much you are going to try. Attitude determines what you see as the possibilities. Attitude determines how well you get along with others. Attitude determines whether you win or lose.

"Attitude is a little thing that makes a big difference."
Winston Churchill, Former Prime
Minister of the United Kingdom

The Importance of Mindset

What is mindset? Mindset is simply one's way of thinking—what makes someone tick. What does it have to do with sports? **Everything!**

There are two mindsets—fixed or growth. Your mindset can push you toward disappointment and failure or can lead you toward success. A fixed mindset eventually operates from fear. In the beginning, you may be confident. You may have developed skills and become good because you loved what you were doing. But eventually, as you remain in a fixed mindset, you live for your results and your results define you. There is a lot of pressure to perform, and you judge whether you are truly good at what you do. You worry that you will not be able to achieve what you dream and when you do not, you judge yourself as having failed. You doubt your capabilities.

ATTITUDE

When you do not get the results that you feel you should, you might come up with excuses as to why you didn't do better. You blame the coach, the conditions, the course, your equipment. Whatever happened just was not fair! You obsess over results, worry about how you will do, and fear that you will not achieve what you should. You need to beat so-and-so. Rather than finishing poorly, you quit. You love being the best and fall apart when you are not.

On the other hand, with a growth mindset, you are filled with optimism and a sense of opportunity. A growth mindset embraces love—a love for what you are doing and a passion for your sport. In a growth mindset, it is all about the process. You can find success in anything you do. You do not have to be perfect because mistakes are part of the learning curve. As long as you are learning from your mistakes, then it is a good thing. You accept challenges and you like competing against someone better than you. It is okay to be a little fish in a big pond because it is about improving and getting better at skills you want to master. You do not have to *be the best*, but you just try to *do your best*. A growth mindset gives you the freedom to grow.

At the Olympics in 1972, in the first run of slalom, I told myself, *Just do the best you can!* I concentrated on putting my best effort into the run because I was in a growth mindset. The result was that I won the first run by 3 hundredths of a second! But that was not the end of the race, and I had another run to go.

Going into the second run, I switched to a fixed mindset. All I could think about was winning a gold medal. I thought about the girls that I wanted to beat. I worried that I would make a mistake and I stressed that I would not be able to repeat what I had done first run. With every thought, I could feel myself choking and feel my muscles getting tighter.

As I was inspecting the course for the second run, I realized that I would not ski well if I kept thinking this way. I told myself,

Come on B.A.! You've got to change how you're thinking, because right now this is not working!

The first thought I had was, *I'm just going to do the best I can. I will focus on putting my best effort into it because that's all I can do. And that is enough.*

The second thought I had was, *If the French girls can win, I can, too!* That built up my confidence.

The third thought I had was what my dad had told me two years before at the World Championships. There, before the second run, I was getting really nervous, so I went up to my dad and told him that. He said, "I always thought you were the 'cool cucumber' in the family!" So, I reminded myself, *I'm the 'cool cucumber' in the family!*

My last thought was, *I've already won the first run of an Olympic slalom race. No matter what happens, I can always be proud of myself for that.* Once I focused on that instead of the results, I calmed down.

In the second run, I lost by one hundredth of a second, but, overall, I won by two-hundredths. With the growth mindset, I did not choke but I gave myself the freedom to ski.

When you are facing a challenge, check to see if you are focusing on the results. If you are, then change it! Instead, tell yourself, *I'm just going to do the best I can!* Remind yourself, *No matter how this comes out, I can do it. With practice, I'll get better.* In a growth mindset, you can have fun, no matter how you do!

Positive or Negative?

When I first made the U.S. Ski Team in the late sixties, my coach recommended that I read a book by Dr. Maxwell Maltz called *Psycho-Cybernetics*. It was an incredible book! One of the things that I learned was how the subconscious mind believes anything you tell it, especially if you send that message with feeling.

From that point on, I decided that I would eliminate the word "can't" from my vocabulary. I made up my mind that I would tell my subconscious that I *could* do whatever I desired, even when my conscious mind knew otherwise. My message was always, "You can do this!"

After that, I was conscious of how I looked at things. Did I see the glass as half-full or half-empty? I came to the conclusion that if my subconscious mind was going to believe anything I told it and couldn't distinguish between what was true and what was false, I would just tell it how capable I was. I would always feed it *positive information*.

My messages became, *I may not be able to do this as well as I'd like to, but I can do this!* Or, *No matter what happens, I should be all right!* Or, *I know I have the skills to win. I don't know if that will happen, but I do know I am capable of it.*

I felt that if what I wanted to do was to win races, I might as well tell my subconscious mind I could, even when I didn't truly believe that was possible. The interesting thing that took place was that by sending these ideas to my subconscious mind, I actually started believing in myself more. I actually started to believe these thoughts!

Positive Thoughts...

...About Having Fun

Years ago, I was at a ski race for J-IV youngsters (the 11- and 12-year-old division) in the Northern Vermont Council. As the parents watched their children competing, one parent shared his thoughts: "If these kids are having fun, they're just not working hard enough!"

That could not be further from the truth! If those kids were *not* having fun, I would suggest that they pack up their skis and go do something else. When a sport is no longer enjoyable for an athlete, some serious questions need to be asked. That's not to say that a sport will be fun every single minute of every single day, but for an athlete to do his best, he must experience an overall enjoyment for the sport in which he is participating.

To experience the high energy and positive emotions that lead to excellence in competition, athletes must enjoy what they're doing. When a competitor is excited, happy, focused, and truly enjoying the moment, performing to the best of her ability is possible.

"People only do their best at things they truly enjoy. It is difficult to excel at something you don't enjoy."
Jack Nicklaus, Pro Golfer and Golf Legend

. . . About Winning

I assume that the majority of people who participate in sports want to win. That's a given. But someone who emphasizes that winning is everything and focuses only on the results is on the wrong track.

I tried to convince a coach of that very idea. He responded, "You can't tell me that every time Michael Jordan steps onto the basketball court, he's not thinking about winning!"

I'm sure that every time Michael Jordan stepped onto the basketball court, he wanted to win, but I doubt that was the main idea that he was thinking about. Michael Jordan played basketball because he *loved* basketball and loved to see the basketball swish through the net. He thought about outwitting the other

ATTITUDE

players and executing the skills he needed to make baskets so that he would be able to help his team win. His focus was NOT on winning the game!

Some athletes make similar connections by saying things like, "Winning is good; losing is bad," or, "Winning equals value, while losing equals worthlessness." In fact, this is a definite commentary about the state of professional sports today. "Winning is succeeding; losing is failing," and "Winners are better than other athletes; losers are less than other athletes."

I lost a lot more races than I ever won, but I felt that every time I had mastered a challenge, I had won. Every time that I had improved in some way, I had won. When I had done my best, I had won. But I also knew that winning was neither good nor bad; it was just a part of the sport.

There is always success in every athletic endeavor. The important thing is to find it. Acknowledge the things that went well because whatever you focus on is what you will get more of. It is better to emphasize the things that you are doing well and simply allow the rest to come. If you emphasize what went wrong, however, you will only reinforce that negative habit.

In a sixty-gate course, if I had only skied one turn well, that was the turn I thought about. I didn't care so much about the other fifty-nine because I knew that if I had performed well in one turn, I could do well in two, and then three, and then four, and so on, until I was skiing most of the course well. That one turn was the success that I needed to emphasize.

"Success is peace of mind, which is a direct result of self-satisfaction in knowing you did your best to become the best you are capable of becoming."
John Wooden, Former UCLA Basketball Coach and Teacher

. . . About Making Mistakes

Mistakes are part of improving. An athlete who feels that he can't make a mistake will never get better. In order to become a more skilled athlete, you need to try things that are not in your comfort zone. If you always perform the skills in which you are confident, you will always stay the same.

On the other hand, if you speed up, if you jump higher, if you press harder, and if you throw faster, your timing will be different from what you are used to, so you will make mistakes. Mistakes simply give you feedback on figuring out how to adjust to new circumstances.

When you're playing a game like field hockey and you miss stopping the ball from going out of bounds, let the disappointment of missing the ball go. If you scold yourself and dwell on that mistake, then it will create a domino effect of negative thoughts and emotions—you will lose focus, your emotions will switch over to unpleasant feelings, and your energy will be used up in berating yourself over what you should have done. In the meantime, the game will have moved on without you.

Instead, let that miss go and get right back into the game! Remember that everyone makes mistakes, playing perfectly is not attainable, and mistakes are an indication that you're trying something more so that you can improve. When you have done your best and are still making mistakes, you cannot ask for anything more. The important concept is to pursue perfection so that you can catch excellence.

"If you're not making mistakes, then you're not doing anything. I'm positive that a doer makes mistakes."
John Wooden, Former UCLA Basketball Coach and Teacher

ATTITUDE

... About Accountability

I learned the importance of practicing with purpose and drive during the first year I went to Chile for training with the U.S. Ski Team. We were running giant slalom. I flew off a bump and thought my pants had ripped, so I skipped the next gate.

When I got to the bottom of the course, my coach reamed me out. "I don't ever want to see you missing a gate like that again!" he said. "If you're going to run the course, run it like it means something. If you can't put your all into the course, don't run it at all!"

He was right. In practice, you develop the exact same attitude that you will have during a competition. If you give up in practice, then it will be a lot easier to give up when you compete.

Thanks, Chuck. It was a lesson well learned!

"The harder you work, the harder it is to surrender."
Vince Lombardi, former football coach of the Green Bay Packers

---

... About Developing Habits

A lesson that I learned from my dad was, "You only get out of something what you're willing to put into it."

His formula was really pretty simple:

- Be in the best possible shape you can be in;
- Pay attention to the details, like making sure your equipment is properly taken care of all of the time; and
- Practice, practice, practice!

He really didn't care whether or not we ever competed in the Olympics. In fact, Dad never dreamed that we would be world-famous when we were youngsters. The lesson he wanted us to learn was that in order to do our best, we had to work hard at it. Excellence requires effort.

Dad did feel that in order to do the best we could in any sport, we had to train more than on weekends. In order to perfect our skills, they had to be repeated over and over and over again, hundreds and hundreds of times, until they became habit.

At the same time, if we had developed a bad habit, the process would take three whole years to correct it and turn it into a new habit. In the first year, we would understand what the bad habit was and recognize when we were doing it. In the second year, we focused on understanding what new movements and skills were needed in the new habit and to practice them until they became natural. Finally, the third year was when our new skill could be accomplished without conscious thought of what had to occur.

Looking back, I'm not so sure it takes three whole years to change a bad habit into a good habit, but I fully realized that the process takes time, which also relieves the stress and pressure of having to improve quickly.

Doing the Best That You Can

A person cannot expect any more from herself than her best. If she's done her best, and she's finished last, so be it. She couldn't have done any better. One has to give herself the freedom to experience her best at whatever level that puts her. The important thing is not to be the best, but to do her best.

My goal was always to do my best. The first year I went to Europe with the U.S. Ski Team to race in the World Cup races, there were six slaloms. At the start of every race, I told myself, *I'm just going to do my best.*

In the first five races, I fell. But after each of those races, I asked myself if I had done my best. Each time, I really felt that I had. I felt that I was moving to a different level and that I was going faster than I was used to. I felt that I would eventually catch up with my timing. In the sixth slalom, I finished fifth.

Before you begin any performance, no matter what it is, tell yourself, *I'm just going to do the best I can!* Know that your best at that particular time may be different from your best on a different day or at another time. Yet, also know that whatever your best is under those conditions, at that time, that was the best that you could do and that doing your best was enough.

"If a man does his best, what else is there?"
George S. Patton, U.S. Army General, WWII

Concentrate on the Skills: Let the Results Take Care of Themselves

Another lesson I learned from my dad was that if you concentrate on the skills, the results will take care of themselves. Sometimes I would look at other racers and think, *I'll never be as good as they are!*

But then I would remember Dad's advice and concentrate on the particular skill I wanted to improve. Perhaps it meant kicking my legs up behind me in the start so I could open the wand with my ankles and literally have every part of my body already on the course except my ankles and feet. Or perhaps it meant skiing a tighter line. There were lots of skills that I wanted to work on. As I made improvements in each of them, I skied faster and faster. Indeed, the results really did take care of themselves.

Concentrating on the results actually backfires for a couple of reasons. First, we cannot control what someone else does. We can only control what we do. Therefore, emphasizing the result "I'm going to win this game!" does not work. You never know how someone else will perform.

Second, concentrating on the results puts more pressure on the person who wants to perform. Thinking about the outcome will only result in nervousness, increased fear, and more tension, which does not allow a person to perform to the best of his ability. Concentrating on the results moves an athlete out of the zone and away from achieving close to his potential.

The 3 Rs to Controlling Negative Attitudes

Getting negative attitudes under control is a three-step process which can be mastered with practice. The steps are (1) recognize the negativity, (2) respond by saying "STOP!" and (3) replace the negative attitude with a positive one.

Recognize the negativity

If you have participated in sports with a negative attitude, changing your thoughts will take time and practice. The first step is to catch yourself in the act. When you form habits, you don't even realize that you're doing it. The thought is an automatic response to the situation. So, the first thing to do is to make a commitment to change and become aware of the negative thoughts.

As you begin, you may ask for help from family, friends, coaches, and others who will recognize the negativity that you want to change. You can also send a message to your subconscious mind to be on the lookout for negative ideas.

The important thing is to listen to yourself. At first, some of the negativity may slip by you. Later, as you think about what's happened, you'll realize, *That was a negative thought!* As you become more alert to those negative thoughts and when they are happening, you'll begin to recognize them in the exact moment when they occur.

Respond by saying "STOP!"

The moment you recognize a negative idea, shout "STOP!" Of course, you don't literally have to shout it because using your inner voice and sending the message to your brain is just as effective. This command is amazingly successful. It grabs attention and upsets the negative process to which you have become accustomed. At this point, you will be able to catch your breath and move on to the next step.

Replace the negative attitude with a positive one

Now that you've identified the negative attitude and successfully stopped it, consciously replace it with a positive idea. It could be as simple as replacing a thought like, *I hate this practice!* with a statement like, *This is so much fun!* Sometimes, when you truly feel like you *do* hate what you're doing in the moment, even though you know that it is necessary and will benefit you, continue to change your thought to how much fun it is because it will help your attitude in the long run. With this change of attitude, you will change your feelings, practice will become more bearable, you will perform better, and you will gain more from the exercise.

HIKE THE COURSE

In what areas do you notice that you have a negative attitude? Complete the exercises on the next two pages to identify your negative attitudes and the positive attitudes with which you can replace them.

How to Gain the Competitive Edge Worksheet

Identifying Negative Attitudes

My Attitude About My Sport: What do you think of your sport? What are the things you like about your sport? The things you dislike? What's the best thing about it? The worst thing?

My Attitude About How Much I Enjoy My Sport: What do you enjoy about your sport? What don't you enjoy about it?

My Attitude About Winning: What do you think about winning? How important is it? How does it relate to your success or failure? Your value? Is it good or bad? How do you perceive yourself if you've lost?

My Attitude About Making Mistakes: What do you say to yourself when you make a mistake? Is making mistakes an okay thing? What do you think about perfection?

My Attitude About Accountability: How much are you willing to put into training? How much do you prepare for competition?

My Attitude About Developing Habits: How do you feel about practicing the same thing over and over and over again?

My Attitude About Doing the Best I Can: Do you always do your best? When do you not do your best?

My Attitude About Concentrating on the Skills: What do you think about when you consider the results? Which do you think about more—skills or results?

How to Gain the Competitive Edge Workbook

Controlling Negative Attitudes

After completing the previous page, write down any negative attitudes that you have identified using the chart below. Record the positive attitude that you have chosen to replace the negative attitude with.

THOUGHTS	NEGATIVE ATTITUDE	POSITIVE ATTITUDE REPLACEMENT
About my sport . . .		
About enjoying my sport . . .		
About winning . . .		
About making mistakes . . .		
About being accountable . . .		
About developing habits . . .		

THOUGHTS	NEGATIVE ATTITUDE	POSITIVE ATTITUDE REPLACEMENT
About doing the best I can . . .		
About concentrating on skills . . .		
Other thoughts . . .		

The Zones: Comfort, Risk, Danger

Another way to look at this is through your zones—the comfort, risk, or danger zones. In your comfort zone, you know what you are doing and you are at ease with your surroundings. There is no tension because this is your place of contentment and your place of familiarity. In sports, it is where you are most confident and sure of your skills, where you believe in yourself, and where you know you will be successful. You can do whatever is asked of you over and over and over with no tension, no questions, and no doubt.

For some athletes, the comfort zone may be very small. This is especially true when a competitor is learning a new sport or a new skill. As an athlete gains confidence, the comfort level will be greater.

When I was 19, I was one of several Vermonters who was being honored with a dinner and an award. We each were expected to give a few remarks as we accepted our gifts. My comfort zone was miniscule when it came to speaking to a group in public! My sister received her award right before me.

I was terrified to get up in front of the crowd and I could barely speak! All I was able to say was, "Thank you. Marilyn has said everything I was going to say!" and then I quickly sat down. I will never be the world's best public speaker, but now I can hold my own. A few years ago, I received an award from the Vermont Alpine Racing Association. I was three-quarters of the way through dinner when it occurred to me that I should be prepared to say something. On that occasion, I spoke without notes and had no speech prepared ahead of time. Later, I heard one of the athletes say that he was completely inspired by my talk. My comfort zone for speaking definitely has grown.

The risk zone pushes you beyond your comfort. This is where you learn new skills. You don't know everything, but you are willing to try. There may be feelings of trepidation, anxiousness, caution, and nervousness. This is your uncertain zone, although you are still willing to take some risks. This is where you feel challenged, but excited. The risk zone is where you improve. The risk zone is the learning zone.

The danger zone is where you become defensive, terrified, and anxious to the point of shutting down. In the danger zone, there is no learning, no development of new skills, and no improvement. The danger zone is where our fears take over. Rational thought disappears. The danger zone is full of red lights and a tremendous desire for escape. For example, I have always viewed the downhill skiing event to be the scariest because it is the longest, fastest, and straightest run. On my "normal" days of running downhill, I was located in the danger zone!

How to Gain the Competitive Edge Worksheet

The Zones – Comfort, Risk, and Danger

The point of this exercise is to understand what lies within each of your zones—comfort, risk, and danger. This is your starting point.

Consider the various facets of your sport. Think about the aspects that feel really comfortable to you, those that feel like there is some risk involved but are generally positive, and those parts that you know get your hackles up, make you feel defensive, cloud your judgment, make you wish you were anywhere else.

Decide on the size of each zone based on your considerations. Do you perform a lot in your comfort zone or your risk zone? Do you work only a little in your danger zone? Make the size of the zones reflect the quantity of time you perform there.

Put each component into the zone that best represents your sense of relative comfort, risk, or danger. To improve, you will want to move out of your comfort zone and into your risk zone. If you move into your danger zone, you've gone too far and won't improve at all. When you first learn a new skill, your comfort zone may be quite small. But as you gain more skill and confidence, your comfort zone will expand. Eventually the things that were in your danger zone will move into your risk zone. The zones constantly evolve.

HOW TO GAIN THE COMPETITIVE EDGE WORKSHEET

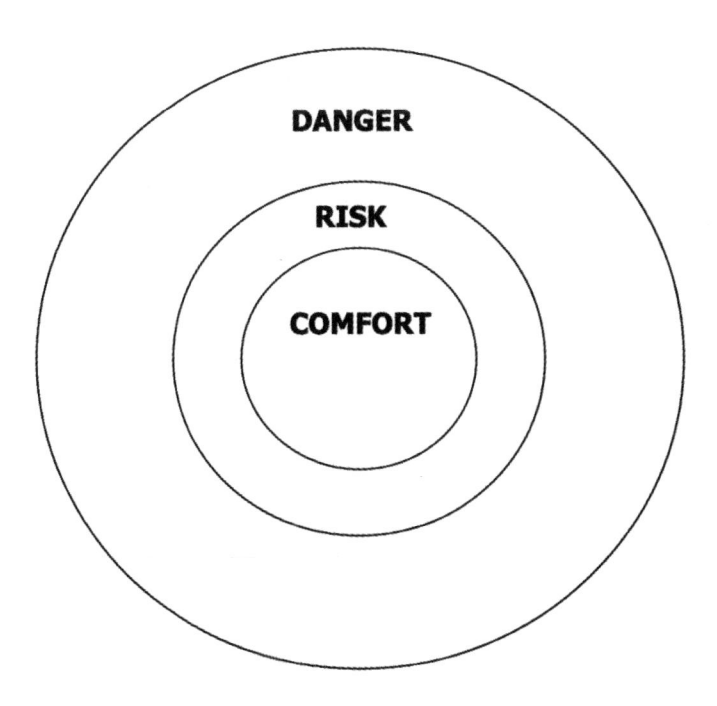

DANGER

RISK

COMFORT

Material adapted from a handout from Marylyn Wentworth in a class by the National School Reform Consortium and Teacher Study Group Coaches Institute in August, 2001.

CHAPTER 10

Beliefs

The law of belief states that whatever we believe to be true, especially when it is accompanied by emotion, will become reality for us. If you believe that you are the second best, you will be second best. Furthermore, others will accept you as second best because that is how you present yourself.

It's the common question, "Which came first—the chicken or the egg?" Do we believe what we see? Or do we see what we already believe? Most often, because we already believe something to be true, that is what we see.

When I was younger and had been racing for a few years, I believed I would never be better than second, if that. Marilyn was so good—she beat all the girls and boys! But at the age of ten, we had a lollipop race at Smugg's and I beat Marilyn! But my belief was so strong that she was better than me, I wondered if the timer had made a mistake.

Marilyn's belief was that she was the best. She was a perfectionist in everything she did and often was the best—the best in sports, the best in school, the best in picking blackberries! One year when I was thirteen and she was fourteen, we were part of the Northern Vermont Council teams. Marilyn fully believed she was going to win, but she had hurt her knee the week before. She was shocked when I beat her and won!

To overcome my belief that I was only second best, I kept plugging away, working on the skills I wanted to master. I considered that every time I performed a skill well, that was a win, even if it was one turn out of 50. Eventually, I improved in slalom so that sometimes I would win and sometimes Marilyn would win. But I began to believe in my ability to do well in slalom. In the next years, the same thing happened in giant slalom, until my confidence in that event grew as well.

The Conscious vs. the Subconscious Mind

Our mind also has a great deal of influence on what we believe to be true. Some of those beliefs are a result of the workings of our conscious mind. As we became aware of our surroundings, our family, how others treated us, etc., our beliefs about ourselves began to form. First, something happened; then, we analyzed or reacted to it; and finally, an opinion was formed. For instance, as a child, if others could not catch you when you played tag, you might have formed the belief that you were a fast runner.

The conscious mind, however, only makes up about 5% of our mind. It's like the tip of an iceberg. The remaining portion, about 95%, is subconscious. Because that part of our mind is so much bigger, it also has much more power. The subconscious mind does not analyze facts—it accepts as true whatever you feed into it, especially when those thoughts are accompanied with emotion.

This is both good and bad. It's good when your conscious thoughts and beliefs line up with your subconscious thoughts and beliefs, and you want all of those things to come true. It's bad when you have no idea what your subconscious beliefs are, and they differ from what you wish to be true.

For instance, when I was competing on the World Cup circuit, I knew I wanted to win every race I competed in. Yet, subconsciously, the message was just the opposite (I did not want to win!) because the subconscious mind knew that I did not like to be noticed. I was extremely uncomfortable with standing in the spotlight. I am an introvert. I loved being part of the U.S. Ski Team, but I was not comfortable having people know who I was. Having people stare at me when I received my award on the first-place podium was intimidating. That subconscious idea held much more power. So, placing second or third was okay, but coming in first was much riskier in my belief system.

As I look back on my career, I realize that in my eight years on the World Cup circuit, I won three races plus the Olympic slalom, but I placed in the top ten over 40 times. It wasn't that I wasn't capable of winning more, it was that, subconsciously, I didn't want to experience the uncomfortable feelings of having people know me and stare at me—just me!

One year, in Val d'Isere, France our first two World Cup races were a slalom and a giant slalom. I finished second in both races, which put me tied in the lead for the overall title for the World Cup. I remember a reporter asking me how I felt and what I was hoping for the rest of the season. When he asked me how I felt, I never told anyone what popped into my head. What I really was thinking was, "I can't wait for next weekend, because I know I won't be in the lead then!" My ideal season would be to stay close to the lead and then win the overall title in the last race of the season. I was that uncomfortable with being the center of attention. Did I want to do well? YES! Did I want to be the racer that the media focused on? NO!

```
          /\
         /  \
        / 5% \   ┌──────────────┐
       /_____\  │ Conscious    │
      /  \  /\\  │ Mind         │
     /\  /\/  \\ └──────────────┘
    /  \/      \
   /    \       \
  /              \
 /      95 %      \  ┌──────────────┐
/                  \ │ Subconscious │
/_____\│ Mind         │
                     └──────────────┘
```

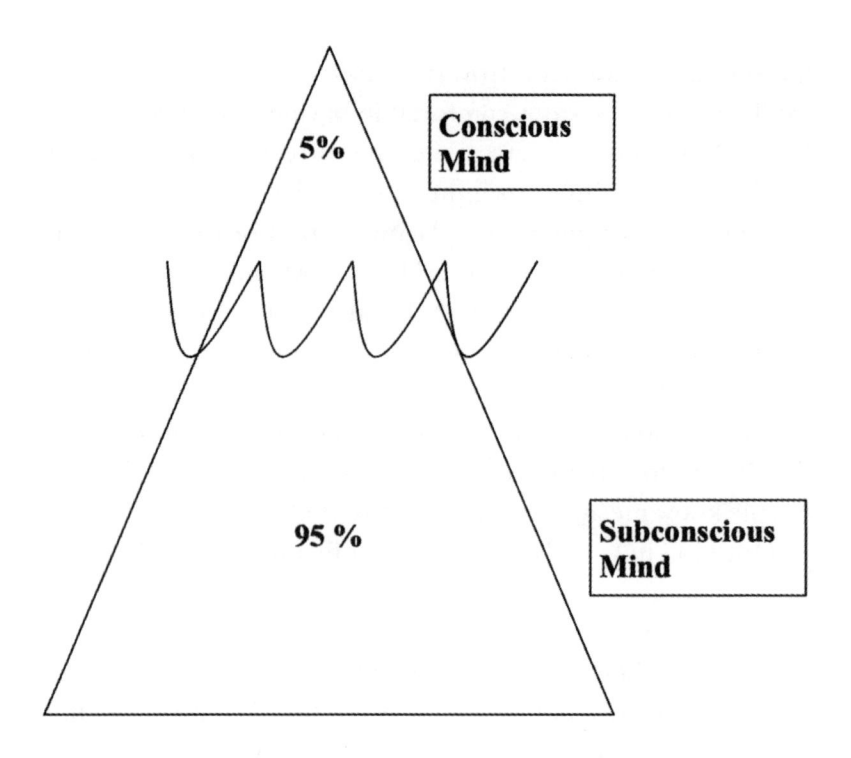

Belief In Yourself

Many of the fears that an athlete experiences all stem from a lack of belief in himself. His thoughts run something like this:

How could I be as good as _____ (fill in the blank)?
After all, my body could never be as good as_____
my training could never be as good as _____
my coaching could never be as good as _____
my equipment is not as good as_____
my ability could never be as good as_____

. . . and on, and on, and on.

The fear that we are just not good enough—that we're not capable, that we can't measure up to what someone else can do, etc.—paralyzes our chances for doing. To be mentally tough, you have to believe in your ability.

If you don't believe in your ability, you have to pretend that you believe in your ability until it becomes true. Anyone who lacks a belief in himself will not perform to his potential. The results may not always come out the way that you would like them to, but you must believe that you are capable of getting those results.

As a ski racer and a new arrival on the European circuit, I looked at the French, German, Austrian, and Swiss racers in awe. But then my thoughts turned to, *What is different about them? What do they have that I don't? What do they do differently from me that make them better?*

My conclusion was, *Nothing! They put their pants on one leg at a time just like me! I've trained just as hard as they have. I'm just as strong as they are.* It sounds kind of corny, but I had this vision of getting dressed that drove home the idea that I was really no different from them.

Another thought that helped to convince my subconscious mind that I was capable and that I could achieve the next level was, *If she can do it, I can, too!* Even when I watched an athlete perform feats that I thought were amazing, I would think, *If she can do it, I can, too!*

The Law of Expectations

In the next chapter on goals, I introduce the law of expectations which suggests that whatever we think or expect to come true, probably will. Setting goals is a wonderful way to begin the process of mental preparation and to set in motion the psychology of achievement. But whether or not you realize those goals is also dependent on whether or not you expect you can accomplish those goals.

At this point, whether or not you believe you can achieve those goals doesn't matter. The important step here is to identify whether or not you believe you can reach those goals. If you realize your aspiration doesn't match your expectation, you can do something about it. You have the freedom to change it.

You could decide that your ambition is too much and change your goal. Or you could decide, *No! That goal is important to me. It's something I really want to accomplish!* Then you need to change your expectation and see yourself as capable of accomplishing that target.

Some people assume that the expectation is reality or what's really genuine. In fact, the only reason the expectation is true is because that is how we perceive it.

CHAPTER 11

Goals

When it comes to mental preparation, one may wonder, *Goals? Everybody has set goals in their lives. How important are they? Wouldn't people get things done anyway, even without setting goals?*

A goal is something for which to strive, something that you'd like to accomplish. Yes, things would get done, even without goals. But goals are like the title in a recipe. Goals describe what you want to accomplish, just as the title tells you what the recipe makes. You could follow the recipe and make a good product. But, without the title, you're guessing what the product might be. The title helps you prepare mentally for what you will be making. Goals help focus your efforts.

For years now, Cochran's Ski Club has prepared for the upcoming season with fall training. Often, one of those days was spent on a hike. Years ago, the hike was up Camel's Hump, a favorite for our family. Among the group was my four-year-old son, Ryan; my six-year-old daughter, Caitlin; my sister, Lindy; her six-year-old son, Robby; and myself.

After hiking 1.3 miles, we stopped for our second rest and snack. It was obvious to me that we weren't going to hike another 2.1 miles to the top, or even reach the meadow, which was three-tenths of a mile from the top. That was okay because my goal was to be outside on a beautiful day, get some exercise, and have fun together.

Then the kids started talking about how cool it was going to be at the very top and that they might see the airplane wing from a wreckage that happened back in the '40s. Lindy and I warned them that we probably wouldn't make it all the way to the top, but that they could keep going. We'd catch up after we finished cleaning and packing back up after snack time.

Lindy eventually overtook the boys and hiked with them all the way to the top. I lagged behind, but finally caught up with Caitlin. We hiked until we got tired and cold and then finally turned around. I never dreamed that little four-year-old Ryan could hike all the way to the top of Camel's Hump! As he later told me, "I knew I could do it and I did!"

When Lindy and I had suggested that we probably wouldn't make it all the way to the top, Ryan and Robby both set a goal that they would. They knew that they had to hike faster, and they were determined that they were going to do it.

Without setting that goal, the boys would have continued to play their way up the mountain—climbing boulders, finding treasures, hiding, and jumping out. Those goals would have been fine, except that they really wanted to get to the top. Once they decided that, they began to truck! They were focused.

What impressed me more than anything was how much achieving that goal meant to them. They bubbled with pride that they had hiked to the top of Camel's Hump! Reaching a goal does indeed increase your self-worth.

Whether we realize it or not, setting goals is something we do every day from the time we get up (Do we want to jump out of bed for an early start or do we hit the snooze button for 10 more minutes of sleep?), to what clothes we wear (Do we dress to make a certain impression?), to what we eat (Do we eat nutritiously or eat something quick and easy?), to what we do throughout the day (Do we want to do anything special today?).

Why Set Goals?

Most people don't take the time to think about the goals they're choosing. But life's funny. Life gives you what you ask for and what you expect. No one ever made a six-figure salary when all he expected to earn was $30,000. If your goal is to develop the skills to be good enough to make it to the Olympic try-outs, you will probably never make it to the Olympics. If your goal is to make it to the play-offs, you probably won't become a state champion.

Earning $30,000, making it to the Olympic try-outs, and competing in the play-offs are all legitimate goals. But the important thing to think about is the goals you've chosen and whether or not those are the goals that you really want to achieve. Sometimes, the goals we set are things that we believe we can achieve. We don't go for more because we don't believe we can accomplish those goals.

Napoleon Hill quoted these lines from a great poet in his book, *Think and Grow Rich*:

"I bargained with Life for a penny,
And Life would pay no more,
However I begged at evening
When I counted my scanty store.

"For Life is a just employer,
He gives you what you ask,
But once you have set the wages,
Why, you must bear the task.

> *"I worked for a menial's hire,*
> *Only to learn, dismayed,*
> *That any wage I had asked of Life,*
> *Life would have willingly paid."*

The most important goal that an athlete can set for himself is to do the best he can, no matter what the situation. Then, there are no limits. Life will take you as far as you can go.

Goals help you decide what you really want to accomplish. Goals help you expand your dreams. Goals help you stretch your limits. With goals, you know where you want to go. In that case, when you do stray from the path, you'll recognize that and make a conscious decision to correct yourself or change goals.

The Process: How Do You Set Goals?

STEP ONE

To launch a journey far beyond your imagination, ask, *What do I really want to accomplish?* Don't worry about how to do it, just figure out what you want to do. In fact, if you ask yourself this question before you go to bed and then sleep on it, your subconscious mind will go to work to figure out what you do want to accomplish, perhaps even by morning. Our minds work at two different levels—we tell our conscious mind what we want to accomplish, and our subconscious mind figures out how to make it happen.

This may seem difficult to believe but give it a try. You probably have solved a problem this way. It's worked for me when I've tried to figure out plumbing problems in my house, when I can't remember someone's name, or when I'm trying to figure out how to do a math problem. Whenever I have a problem, I ask myself, *What can I do to* . . . Then, I forget about it. Ideas pop into my head when I'm least expecting them.

STEP TWO

After you know what you really want to accomplish, write them down. Thinking about goals allows them to come and go more easily. Often, when we've had a great thought without writing it down, the only thing we remember is that we had a great thought.

The subconscious mind is the keeper of all our fears and beliefs and will sabotage our efforts unless we mean what we say. I'd like to lose weight and become more fit, so I'm trying to change my eating habits and work out three times a week. The longer I've been at this, the easier it becomes to think, *I'm so tired! I don't have time today! I need to eat something sweet! I'm still hungry! My knee hurts!* Those thoughts will sabotage my efforts (and sometimes do!) when I don't recommit to my goal daily.

Our subconscious also waits to see how serious we are. If we have a thought that we'd like to go to the moon and that's the one and only time our subconscious hears about it, our mind makes a judgment that that thought didn't matter and didn't have any substance to it. The subconscious won't take action unless it's convinced that we're serious and that the goal is important! Writing our goals down gives our subconscious mind the message that we are committed. When our subconscious mind is convinced that we mean business, we will begin to produce ideas that will lead to the actual achievement of our goals.

STEP THREE

As you begin to list your goals, write lots and lots of them. There are several reasons for this. Different goals take different lengths of time to accomplish. When you write lots of goals, you will complete some within a day, a month, or a season, while others will take a year or longer.

When I was thirteen, I met several top ski racers from the U.S., including Billy Kidd who had just won a silver medal at the Olympics in Innsbruck, Austria. I was so impressed! They were such great skiers, yet they were nice. At that moment, I decided that I wanted to be like them. I wanted to be one of the best skiers in the U.S. and race in the Olympics. That goal took me eight years to achieve.

Another reason for setting many goals is that after you accomplish a goal, it loses its power or purpose. It no longer carries any meaning for you. This concept was one that I experienced as an athlete but did not understand until much later.

After winning the gold medal at the Olympics, I was surprised to recognize how I felt. I had just done the most amazing thing in my life and had gone through great lengths to accomplish this goal for many years—sprinted up hills, religiously followed a weight-lifting routine, practiced six hours a day regardless of the weather conditions, even in rain, sleet, and blizzards. I had sweated and pushed myself to the point where my lungs gasped for air and my muscles burned with pain.

Yet, after I won at the Olympics, I felt a let-down and a sense of disappointment. I asked myself, *Is this all there is?* I expected to feel exhilarated, like I was floating 10 feet off the ground!

Don't get me wrong. I was very excited that I had won. But I didn't feel like I was floating. What I realize now is that I had achieved my goal, but I had no goals beyond that point on which to focus. Once I accomplished that goal, it no longer had meaning for me. It no longer had power and had no other purpose at that moment.

The third reason for setting lots of goals has to do with abundance.

---

*"It's not that people want too much.
It's that they want too little."*
Jack Canfield and Mark Victor Hansen,
Best-selling authors of Dare to Win

If you want to achieve something in life, go for it and do not sell yourself short. I believe that life gives us what we ask for. Just be sure that you're really asking for what you want.

STEP FOUR

Another step in setting goals is to carry them with you. If you mean what you've written, you're committed to them and want to achieve them. That requires you to put them in your face often so your path will become clearer, and your dedication will strengthen. Achieving your goals will just be a matter of time. It will be a matter of "when" rather than "if."

STEP FIVE

I recommend setting lofty goals as well. The lofty goals expand your limits. Let yourself dream! Your intuition will know if that goal is too much for the present. You will become anxious, nervous, and feel like you've bitten off too much. You may just have to "chunk it down."

If I had set a goal at age 13 that, by age 14, I would make the U.S. Ski Team, that would have been too much. I may have become neurotic trying to achieve it. I would have set too lofty a goal for that time frame. But if I "chunked it down" and worked on my skills, I may have been able to make it in two or three years, which is exactly what I did.

STEP SIX

For a goal or goals that are lofty, making a collage may help because adding the sense of sight intensifies your commitment and sends the message that this is possible. Start with clipping articles of people who have accomplished what you would like to do. Find pictures that represent your goals and cut out words or put letters together to form words that remind you of your goals. A collage makes your goal more real, and it is especially powerful when you see it every day.

Another idea is to make a vision movie. The movie should be from one to three minutes long. After identifying what you want to accomplish, create a visual that represents that goal. The skiers with whom I work add a short clip of someone who has mastered that particular skill that they are aiming toward. If they want to make the Olympic team, then they include a picture of the Olympic rings. If they want to win more races, then they take a picture of them on top of a podium. Once your vision movie is complete, then plan to watch it both morning and night to keep the right focus. Watch it the first thing in the morning when you wake up and then again before you go to sleep. Over time, notice how it helps you remain motivated and focused on your goals.

STEP SEVEN

The next step in goal-setting is to keep your goals to yourself. People have a way of shooting goals down. Let the achievement of the goals speak for themselves. Any time you share a goal with someone, if you experience any judgment or criticism, keep quiet, even if that person is your parent, friend, teacher, or coach. On the other hand, if you experience support and encouragement while sharing goals, you may have found a safe environment. In that case, you are welcome to talk about your goals to gain support.

If you wonder if people really treat goals so negatively, just ask someone who has tried to lose a few pounds. The minute that others find out that they are trying to diet, people immediately begin to bake for them, offer them goodies, or tell them, "You don't need to lose weight! Why are you trying to lose weight?"

STEP EIGHT

Whenever I complete a goal, even as simple as finishing a chore, I feel a sense of satisfaction in crossing it off my list. I've also learned that not only do I check it off, but I also write "victory!" Because that is just what it is. A victory!

STEP NINE

Remind yourself often of the most important goal of all for success: Always do the best you can, whatever the situation and whatever the circumstances!

"If you'll not settle for anything less than your best, you will be amazed at what you can accomplish in your lives."
Vince Lombardi, Former football coach of the Green Bay Packers

How to Gain the Competitive Edge Worksheet

Goal-Setting

HOW DO YOU SET GOALS?
(As you complete each step, check it off).

STEP ONE: Ask yourself, *What do I really want to accomplish?* Then sleep on it and wait for an answer to pop into your mind when you least expect it.
My answer:
_____
_____
_____
_____
_____

STEPS TWO AND THREE: Set lots & lots of goals. Write them down.
My goals:
_____
_____
_____
_____
_____

STEP FOUR: Carry them with you. I recommend writing them on an index card & carrying them in your pocket.

STEP FIVE: Write lofty goals.
My lofty goals – my dreams:

_____
_____
_____
_____
_____

STEP SIX: Make a visual. This can be as simple as a collage or more creative like a vision movie.

STEP SEVEN: Keep your goals to yourself.

STEP EIGHT: After accomplishing a goal, write "VICTORY!"

STEP NINE: The most important goal of all for my success is:

_____
_____
_____
_____
_____

Personal Goals and Action Plan

After completing the nine steps in setting goals, it's time to refine them and to give them a tune-up. The "Personal Goals and Action Plan" worksheet will help with this. Goals generally are categorized into (1) long-term, (2) intermediate, and (3) short-term goals.

Long-term Goals

Long-term goals are your lofty goals. What are your dreams? What do you hope to accomplish? When you look ten years ahead, what are you hoping to look back on? Do you want to have competed in the Olympics? Won a gold medal? Be part of a professional baseball, football, basketball, or soccer team? Set a world record? Compete for a Division I college?

Please remember that this is your dream and your goal, not someone else's. Being realistic at this point is not important. This is simply your dream and belief in what you might someday be able to accomplish. Before you can even consider achieving a goal like this, you have to be able to dream it.

Goals, especially lofty goals, are not set in stone. They can be modified whenever you decide to change them.

Intermediate Goals

Intermediate goals are the stepping-stones to the realization of your long-term goals. They may take six months or longer to accomplish but should be achievable. When you consider your intermediate goals, also consider the approximate date when you will accomplish it.

If you decide that your dream is to play professional baseball, what can you do to accomplish that goal? Do you need to improve your batting? Your fielding? Perhaps you're a pitcher. Do you need to work on delivery or on using your legs for more power? From whom can you learn? What books can you read and analyze? How often can you practice? What should you be able to do six months from now that you're currently unable to do?

When you decide what you will be achieving down the road, remember to also include the date when you will have accomplished it.

Short-term Goals

Short-term goals are your goals and your plan of action for today, tomorrow, and the next six months. These are goals that you can and will achieve. Include when you will take this action, where it will happen, and how many times you will do it.

For instance, perhaps to attain your goal of becoming a major league baseball player, you realize that you need to be stronger. Part of your action plan could be that you will work out three to four times per week with free weights at home after you get home from school. This routine might also include cardiovascular fitness and stretching for flexibility.

To improve your technique, you could practice three to four times a week with a friend, parent, or personal coach for a couple of hours. Before you fall asleep at night, you can visualize the movements. Imagine yourself successfully competing as a major league baseball player, wearing the uniform (of the Boston Red Sox, of course!), hearing the crowds chant your name, smelling the peanuts and hotdogs, and feeling the stitches of the baseball in your hand. Make your visualization as real as possible by using as many different senses as possible.

When my dad was about ten, he went to bed with a baseball and practiced holding the grip for different pitches. He eventually became a good pitcher in what was called the Northern League at the time and was even invited by the Red Sox to try out for their team! (By that time, he had gotten married, started his family, and felt that a professional athlete's life was not the life for a family, so he never accepted their offer.)

When you take action, your subconscious mind will be impressed with your dedication and will try to make your dream come true, especially when your body and soul scream about how much fun all of this is!

Results-Oriented vs. Skills-Oriented Goals

Besides your long-term, intermediate, and short-term goals, another consideration is what type of goal it is. When most people think of goals, they consider the results-oriented goals. That is to say, what will the ultimate result look like? Perhaps it means being on the Olympic team, winning a gold medal, being part of a professional team, setting a world record, or beating other competitors.

Lofty goals are often results-oriented. But the difficulty with these goals is that they are influenced by others. You have no control over them. When I won my gold medal, I had no control over what the other competitors would do. I could only control myself. That result was dependent on how the others did.

It's okay for lofty goals to be results-oriented because they are so far in the future. You don't even know who the other players will be that far down the road. By setting the scene for your subconscious mind, if that goal truly is meaningful to you, your body and brain will begin the process of figuring out how you will get there.

Short-term goals need to be achievable, however, so they should be skills-oriented. They have to be something over which you have control. Conditioning programs are skills-oriented. Practicing a technical skill to make it automatic or a habit is skills-oriented. Eating well and getting enough sleep are skills-oriented. The goals you set over those things that you have control are all skills-oriented. The accomplishment of that goal is dependent upon your actions and no one else's.

The intermediate goals can be a mixture of both types. Hoping to qualify for Nationals or All-Stars, for instance, are all legitimate but they are results-oriented goals. Perfecting a start, mastering a movement, or improving fitness are all examples of skills-oriented goals. Be sure to include the mastery of skills-oriented goals in mind as well.

The worksheet on the next page will help you to refine your goals.

How To Gain The Competitive Edge Worksheet

My Personal Goals & Action Plan

I. Long-term goals

In my fondest dream, what would I like to accomplish? What would I like to be doing in [my sport] in five to ten years? Please remember that this is *your* dream and *your* goal—not someone else's. Being realistic is not important. This is simply your dream and belief in what you might someday be able to accomplish.

_____
_____
_____
_____
_____
_____
_____
_____
_____
_____
_____
_____
_____
_____

II. Intermediate goals:

What are the stepping-stones to the realization of my long-term goals? (These goals will take six months or longer to accomplish but should be achievable). Include the goal and approximate date when you will accomplish it.

GOAL	DATE TO COMPLETE

III. Short-term goals:

These are my goals—my plan of action—for today, tomorrow, and the next six months. (These are goals that you *can* and *will* achieve.) Include when you will take this action, where it will happen, and how many times you will do it.

GOAL	WHEN	WHERE	FREQUENCY

The Law of Expectations

The probability of accomplishing your goals will be influenced by the law of expectations. The law of expectations suggests that whatever we think or expect to come true probably will.

Setting goals is a wonderful way to begin the process of mental preparation—to set in motion the psychology of achievement. But whether or not you realize those goals is also dependent on whether or not you expect you can accomplish those goals.

At this point, whether or not you believe you can achieve those goals doesn't matter. The important step here is to identify whether or not you believe you can reach those goals. If you realize your aspiration doesn't match your expectation, you can do something about it. You have the freedom to change it.

You could decide that your ambition is too much and change your goal. Or you could decide, *No! That goal is important to me. It's something I really want to accomplish!* Then you need to change your expectation and to see yourself as capable of accomplishing that target.

Some people assume that the expectation is reality, or what's genuine. In fact, the only reason that the expectation is true is because that is how we perceive it.

> *"If you think you can, you can. And if you think you can't, you're right."*
> Henry Ford, Automotive pioneer

There are essentially two ways to change your expectation. The first is to use affirmations. Chapter 14 covers affirmations in more detail, but an affirmation is simply a positive declaration, stated in the present as if the desired result were already happening.

The first time I realized how powerful affirmations are was when I was working with a young athlete who had moved from my ski club to a different one. She was devastated. She loved her old club and hated her new environment. She didn't like the other competitors or the coaches at all. She used an affirmation to help herself adapt positively to her new club. Her affirmation was simply, "I *love* racing at Smugg's!"

She bombarded her brain with that message. She wrote that message on 20 different index cards and plastered them all over her house. She attached them to her bureau, her bed post, the bathroom mirror, to door jams, lamp shades, notebooks—anywhere and everywhere that she could think of.

When she started, that statement was not true for her at all. But, at the end of two weeks, the mother of one of her friends asked her, "So, how do you like racing at Smugg's?" Her reply came before she had time to even think about it! She blurted out, "I *love* racing at Smugg's!"

At that point, that may have only been partially accurate because she was still torn. Subconsciously, however, she was beginning to act as if it were true. So, before long, it really did become true for her.

The second technique is to visualize achieving your goal. In your head, see yourself successfully mastering the desired result. If you want to qualify for the national championships, imagine yourself there, competing in your sport, and achieving the results that you want.

If you bombard your brain with your affirmations and visualize it becoming a reality on a daily basis, your expectations will change. You will believe that you can do it!

The Disappointment Threshold

The other issue to consider is your disappointment threshold, or the point in which you are disappointed in your results. The first time I raced in the World Cup, I was thrilled to be there. Just finishing was a delight! But, at the height of my success, I was disappointed to finish out of the top five, or maybe even three, especially in slalom.

What is your disappointment threshold? To conquer your lofty goals, you must expect that you can achieve them, and your disappointment threshold must be close to that goal.

"You got to be careful if you don't know where you're going, because you might not get there."
Yogi Berra, former baseball player and coach

How to Gain the Competitive Edge – Worksheet

Goals, Expectations, & Disappointment Threshold

The probability of accomplishing your goals will be influenced by the *law of expectations*. The *law of expectations* suggests that whatever we think or expect to come true, probably will. The *disappointment threshold* is that point at which you are disappointed in your results.

"Sooner or later, those who win are those who think they can."
Richard Bach, best-selling author of
Jonathan Livingston Seagull

For each goal, describe what you expect to happen and where you will be disappointed if you don't reach that goal: *

Goals	Expectation	Disappointment Threshold

HOW TO GAIN THE COMPETITIVE EDGE – WORKSHEET

Goals	Expectation	Disappointment Threshold

*Although there is only space for four goals, remember that Step Three suggests writing lots and lots of goals. This exercise is especially good when considering your long-term (lofty) and intermediate goals. Be sure to consider all of these goals.

CHAPTER 12

The Emotionally Intelligent Athlete

What is Emotional Intelligence?

There is still some debate among scientists about the real definition for emotional intelligence. As I discuss emotional intelligence, I assume that it is an all-encompassing knowledge of emotions. I also presume that it is two-pronged:

Personal competence: Knowing what you feel as it happens (having self-awareness), managing feelings (having the ability to handle emotions and recover), and motivating yourself (creating an inner climate to reach goals and maintain self-discipline); and

Social competence: Recognizing emotions in others (being able to empathize by feeling what another feels) and relationship management (being able to get along with others).

Because emotions drive performance, an athlete's knowledge of emotions and how to handle them is critical.

In sports, personal competence is essential. Some people have a difficult time identifying how they feel. They simply lack the ability to name what they are experiencing. In my work with athletes, when I ask an athlete to identify what they are feeling at the start, for instance, they sometimes will tell me what they think—for example, "I don't want to get beat by so-and-so."

Becoming Emotionally Intelligent

STEP ONE

The first step for an athlete to become emotionally intelligent is to identify emotions and how exactly that feels for them. Look at the list of emotions below. Describe what each emotion feels like. Understand what goes on inside your body with each feeling.

Emotions

Overwhelmed	Glad	Proud
Satisfied	Disappointed	Bored
Shy	Scared	Mad
Anxious	Confused	Ashamed
Angry	Happy	Lonely
Depressed	Disgusted	Hopeful
Confident	Frustrated	Sad
Jealous	Excited	Joyful

Think about what the difference is between being angry and being mad? Is there any difference? What about depressed and sad and bored? The more you are able to identify feelings, the easier it will be to manage your emotions. What emotions can you identify that are not on this list?

STEP TWO

The second step is to relate how you feel under particular circumstances. For example, what do you experience when you're training? Are you excited? Happy? Loving what you're doing? How about when you're competing? Excited? Happy? Loving what you're doing? Nervous? Scared? Anxious? Psyched-out? Bored? Consider various situations and the feelings that accompany each one of those incidents. The more self-aware you become, the easier it will be for you to manage your emotions.

STEP THREE

The third step is to manage your emotions and create an inner climate that enables you as an athlete to achieve success. This chapter begins the process of understanding how to handle your emotions. In the following chapter, I will explain how to control emotions by managing your thoughts.

Social Competence

Although social competence certainly plays a role in sports—for instance, how an athlete gets along with his teammates, his coaches, and others in his life—this chapter was written to help an athlete manage his own stress and emotions regarding competition.

The Brain/Emotion Connection

To understand emotions, one must appreciate what a feeling is. The Latin derivative of emotion is "motere" which means "to move" and "e" which means "away." So, emotion is simply a feeling from which there is movement away. In other words, when we feel an emotion, we want to do something. The greater or more intense the feeling, the greater or more intense the movement.

When we feel happy, we feel exuberant, we smile, and we jump with joy. When we feel angry, we lash out with words or with fists and are ready to fight back. When we are afraid, we crouch in fear, we hide, and we tremble. When we feel depressed, we sleep, we avoid contact with others, and we slow down.

Emotions and Energy

Another matter concerning emotions is that all emotions have different energy levels attached to them. Happiness and anger are both high energy emotions. Fear has a little less energy. Depression has very little, or no energy attached to it. When you look at the grid from the "Evaluating the Inner Climate" worksheet at the end of this chapter, any of the emotions on the lower half do not have much energy attached to them. When an athlete is experiencing these emotions, there is no chance that he will do well. A winning performance is at the mercy of energy.

Feeling vs. Thinking

The human brain has many functions. Two roles it plays in mental preparation are to feel and to think. The human brain is interesting in that it is made up of both a feeling mind and a thinking mind. Usually, these two entities coordinate responses, and our thoughts are linked to our feelings. Once in a while, our responses are so passionate and so powerful that we have an "emotional hijacking" in which the thinking mind gets left behind, and pure emotion takes over. When someone has "lost it" or "blows up at someone" and later can't figure out why they acted the way they did, they've experienced an "emotional hijacking," which is explained by Daniel Goleman in his book, *Emotional Intelligence: Why It Can Matter More Than IQ.*

Goleman explains that, in an emotional hijacking,

"[The emotional mind] proclaims an emergency, recruiting the rest of the brain to its urgent agenda. The hijacking occurs in an instant, triggering the reaction crucial moments before … the thinking brain has had a chance to glimpse fully what is happening, let alone decide if it is a good idea. The hallmark of such a hijack is that once the moment passes, those so possessed have the sense of not knowing what came over them."

The thinking mind, or "head," is the rational mind. It understands by becoming aware of a situation. It mulls over the facts and considers the situation and then comes to an understanding or conclusion.

The feeling mind, or "heart," is the emotional mind. It is impulsive, powerful, and sometimes illogical. The more intense the feeling, the more powerful the emotional mind becomes and the less effectual the rational mind is.

Another interesting element in the battle of the head versus the heart is that knowing something in your head, or having logical reasoning, has less conviction than knowing something in your heart. For example, just ask young athletes why they bought a particular brand of shoes. Most likely, the first reason will be emotionally-based, such as, "I wanted to be cool!"

Also, an athlete who knows in his heart what he is capable of will achieve far more than what the coach perceives to be possible based on talent, size, or athletic ability. No coach can ever tell what an athlete is capable of in his heart.

"It is not the size of a man but the size of his heart that matters."
Evander Holyfield, four-time Heavyweight
Champion of the World

In another chapter, I will explain how the thinking mind and the emotional mind work together and how an athlete can manage emotions by controlling thoughts. Here I would like to give a brief overview of how emotions are connected to the brain.

The Emotional Control Center

The control center for emotions is called the amygdala. These bundles of nerves receive information and analyze the data for its emotional value. While other parts of the brain remember past experiences and the facts accompanying that incidence, the amygdala remembers the emotions that went with the facts.

The emotional mind has two circuits–a longer route which incorporates the rational mind and a short-cut which only includes the feeling mind. When the emotion is intense and powerful, the amygdala is king, conquering all other parts of the brain.

The brain decides which route to take when the amygdala scans all past experiences to evaluate what is happening now compared to anything that happened in the past that was similar. If there is one key element that is familiar, the amygdala calls it a match and floods the brain with that emotion.

That is why some athletes can react badly to an incident while another athlete keeps his head and maintains control of his emotions. Let's say, for example, that a soccer player is about to take a shot to score a goal and gets tripped. That information reaches his brain within milliseconds. If the player ever felt humiliated before, such as when he tripped as a kid and several bullies responded by taunting him, the amygdala will consider that reaction to be a close enough "match" to elicit a similar response of humiliation.

If other experiences of being tormented or pushed also reminded the player of episodes when he had reacted with anger and rage, all those emotions will erupt in an instant before his thinking mind has a chance to analyze what really happened.

If his emotions were passionate and powerful enough, he will experience an "emotional hijacking" where he completely loses all rational thought and jumps up to fight the player, even if his opponent had merely been trying to get the ball and inadvertently tripped him!

In situations in which our natural alarm system is activated, the path is short-circuited from the thalamus directly to the amygdala, which then overrides the thinking brain. Because the amygdala only receives a small amount of information, the conclusion of what is happening is not always accurate. It is, at best, a rough signal. Nevertheless, the athlete reacts with intense emotion and "loses it." That anger and frustration turn quickly to rage. At this point, the athlete may swear at a referee or get in a fight with the opponent. The athlete experiences an "emotional hijacking."

Athletes who experience frequent "emotional hijackings" must understand that their performance is hindered by these reactions. This circuit in our nervous system evolved thousands and thousands of years ago when such a reaction played a huge role in whether or not someone survived. The body was able to react within milliseconds to danger, even before a person understood what the danger was. As those powerful emotions surging within the brain triggered a physical response, the individual would know whether to run, fight, or hide. That reaction could save his life.

Although "emotional hijackings" still affect athletes, today, the athlete is not in danger because the short-circuit nervous system is outdated. In baseball, when a player "suddenly and inexplicably loses the ability to perform even basic functions in assignments he previously excelled in" (Wikipedia), the "emotional hijacking" has a name called "the yips" or "Steve Blass disease," so named after Steve Blass, a major league baseball pitcher who inexplicably lost control of himself after the 1972 season.

Chuck Knoblach, a second baseman for the New York Yankees, was considered by many to be one of the best fielders but also suffered from "the yips" and lost his ability to throw accurately to first. He was never able to gain control of his "emotional hijacking" that gave him the feeling of an overwhelming trauma of failure when throwing to first, so he was eventually moved to the outfield.

"No man can think clearly when his fists are clenched."
George Jean Nathan, American author and drama critic

My Experience at Jackson Hole, Wyoming

When I competed in the sixties and early seventies, I raced in three events, which were the only three events in Alpine racing at the time—slalom, giant slalom, and downhill. Slalom was my favorite by far. Giant slalom was challenging but fun. Downhill was terrifying! I did not like the speed, the turns, or the bumps. Every time I ran it, I prayed that I wouldn't get hurt.

Yet, one year in Jackson Hole, Wyoming, I ran a downhill better than anyone by a large margin—six seconds to be exact. By comparison, that would be even better than Roger Bannister breaking the four-minute-mile barrier. How did I do it? Here is my story:

Because downhills are too dangerous without training, every downhill event has two or three days of practice on the course. This is very different from slalom and giant slalom, which cannot be skied before the race. A competitor may look at the slalom or giant slalom course and study it, but no one can ski the actual gates until the race itself.

Today's downhills are much more structured than they used to be because there are a set number of training runs. Every racer is expected to ski the course from top to bottom. In my era, however, everyone got as many training runs as they could fit in. Racers started when they got to the start and there was no special order. A competitor could run part of the course, stop, watch how others were running that turn, and then ski another section.

In the sixties and seventies, on the day before the competition, officials ran a "non-stop" to be sure every athlete had at least one complete run from start to finish. It was exactly like the race itself—competitors wore their starting bibs and ran in race order. The racers left at minute intervals and the non-stop was timed. Racers prepared their skis as if they were competing. Everything happened as if it were a race day. The only difference was that it was the last official training run.

That year, my teammates and I were put up with families throughout the town of Jackson. On the morning of the non-stop, our coach drove the rental station wagon throughout town and picked up six of us at the various homes where we were staying. It was early morning at about 6:00 AM when our coach picked up the last four girls and we all headed to the mountain that was about 30 minutes away.

I was sitting in the middle seat in the front. The windshield was completely frosted over with the exception of two small circles where the defroster had managed to warm the glass and clear the frost. Because we were in the residential part of town, we had to cross several streets before we got onto the highway. The snowbanks were huge, so in order to see into the street, you had to nose the car out slowly until you could see around the wall of snow.

I noticed that, at our first intersection, our coach drove through the stop sign. I don't know if he just didn't see it or if he figured that no one would be on the streets that early. But, once again at the next intersection, he failed to stop.

We weren't going very fast but, in the second intersection, there was a car coming that had the right-of-way. The other driver couldn't stop and hit us broadside, right behind the passenger seats. No one was seriously hurt but two girls went to the hospital. One girl had stitches over her eye and the other one was checked out for a bump on her head. The rest of us were picked up by another vehicle and taken the rest of the way up the mountain.

I didn't realize it at the time, but I went into shock. In the starting gate, I felt nothing. I wasn't afraid. I wasn't anxious about the speed. I wasn't scared of the bump. I wasn't terrified about going into the air. Nothing. It was as if all of my emotions and beliefs about downhill had been lifted from my body.

I just skied the course. I didn't fight it at all. When I flew off the bump higher than I had ever been in my life, I didn't react. I just landed softly and finished the course. My sister, Marilyn, looked at the scoreboard and told me, "Boy! Did they mess up your time! They have you winning by six seconds!"

When she told me that, I knew that there was no mistake—that really was my time! Then she added, "Well, we'll just have to see what you do tomorrow!"

The next day, I was back to my normal self—afraid, anxious, nervous, and scared. I knew that I hated downhill and wasn't very good at it. So, on race day, I finished six seconds behind the winner.

That was a twelve second spread! In ski racing, if you can cut your time by half a second, you've made a major improvement. Essentially, I had skied the course on race day the same way I had on the non-stop. The only difference was that my emotions were in full control. I was terrified all the way down. I dreaded the bump from the time I left the start. My body fought back with tense muscles, out-of-control thoughts, a pessimistic attitude, and a belief that fully knew that this was one place where I didn't want to be.

The result? A race that was twelve seconds slower!

Potential Achievement vs. Actual Results

How could my results have changed that drastically overnight? How was it possible that I could ski faster than the rest of the field by six seconds on the day of the non-stop?

The answer lies in understanding what my potential was in downhill. When I competed in the non-stop, I competed without negative emotions, beliefs, attitude, or thoughts. I was able to compete by performing the technical skills I had learned up to that point. I skied pretty close to, or fully at, my potential.

Did I have the ability to repeat that on race day? Yes! Potentially. However, when I was back to my normal self and allowed the negative emotions, beliefs, attitude, and thoughts full range, all those things blocked me from reaching my potential.

"Perfection is not attainable. But if we chase perfection, we can catch excellence."
Vince Lombardi, former football coach of the Green Bay Packers

---

Reaching your potential is reaching your perfection. That may not be fully attainable, but loving what you do, believing in yourself, performing with a positive attitude, and entertaining only positive thoughts will allow you to "catch excellence," as Vince Lombardi so eloquently put it.

I only wish that I had figured that out while I was still racing! Maybe I could have won the World Cup!

Your Potential Achievement

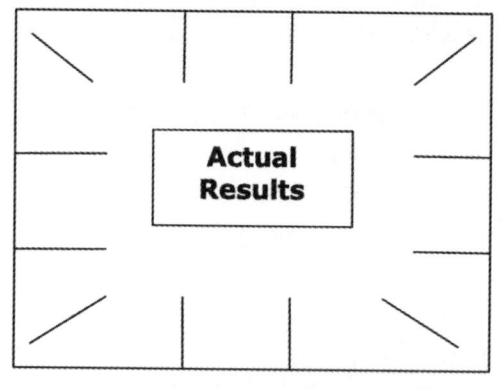

Actual Results

Your Potential Achievement

As seen in the above figure, everyone has a potential achievement level. That is where there is a limit to what is humanly possible, no matter what an athlete does, whether it means improving his strength, fitness, skills, or attitude. Eventually, the record for the mile will be such that no human will ever be able to go faster. That will be potentially what anyone might achieve.

Then there are our individual potential achievement levels. For the majority of us, our actual results are far less than our potential achievement. As seen in the previous figure, there is often a lot of room to improve and move closer to our potential achievement, of which mental preparation can play a huge role.

Sometimes athletes *are* able to come close to their potential. When this happens, they live through a peak experience or, as some may express it, perform in the zone. The psychologist, Mihaly Csikszentmihalyi, describes it as "flow–a state of concentration so focused that it amounts to absolute absorption in an activity." Whether you think of it as having a peak performance, competing in the zone, or flowing, an athlete is totally in tune with the experience and enjoying every second of it. In this state, time seems to stand still.

Emotions: The Driving Force

No matter what else you consider, the driving force behind results is emotions. Emotions fuel performance.

"My weaknesses are my jumps. The reason is that although I land them in practice, when I actually compete or perform, I should let my body go and stabilize my mind better. Also, I need to work on not letting negative thoughts and emotions get to me on the ice."
Oksana Baiul, 1994 Olympic Gold Medalist, Figure Skating

The first step in an action plan to gain control of emotions is to (1) identify what emotions you feel and (2) evaluate the conditions under which they occur. For example, some people perform better when they're training, some rise to the occasion and perform better when they're competing, and some train and compete about the same—it doesn't really make a difference.

Compare all of the emotions you feel in different circumstances. Notice when you do better and identify those feelings on the next page. Notice when you "choke," or don't do as well as you know you can, and identify those feelings as well. When doing this exercise, compare different circumstances, such as:

- Training vs. Competing
- Competing Locally vs. Competing Away

- Singles vs. Doubles
- 500 meters vs. 1000 meters
- Offense vs. Defense
- Take-off vs. Landing
- Slalom vs. Downhill

Some emotions are positive activators, while others are negative activators. The positive activators allow us to move easily, to think clearly, and to remain calm under fire. The positive activators are the emotions we experience when we're having fun and loving what we're doing. They're the emotions that are released when we have a peak performance or compete in the zone.

The negative activators are the negative emotions that create havoc with excellence. Fear, nervousness, jealousy, anger, and anxiety are all negative emotions and, therefore, negative activators.

NEGATIVE ACTIVATORS	POSITIVE ACTIVATORS:
Anger	Having fun
Resentment	Joy
Anxiety	Love
Hate	Determination
Fear	Optimism
Tension	Enjoyment
Negativism	Pride
Threat	Self-challenge
Frustration	Team spirit
Blame	Self-motivation

How to Gain the Competitive Edge Worksheet

Emotions

Emotions affect performance. When someone is experiencing negative emotions, performing well is difficult. We perform best when we experience positive emotions.

Below are words and phrases that describe various emotions. Circle the words or phrases that you experience when you are training. Underline the words or phrases that you experience when you are competing.

bored	frantic	jealous	loving
careless	hesitant	mad	motivated
defeated	nervous	mean	open
depressed	panic	resentment	optimistic
discouraged	scared	rude	hopeful
drained	tense	vengeful	purposeful
futile	threatened	judgmental	secure
hopeless	timid	haughty	tireless
don't care	uncertain	vain	vigorous
lazy	worry	terrified	delight

lost	frustrated	hatred	everything's okay
overwhelmed	impatient	assured	glowing
powerless	manipulative	cheerful	joyful
tired	never satisfied	complete	naturalness
why try?	obsessed	confident	playful
ashamed	pushy	daring	radiant
disappointed	reckless	decisive	warm
embarrassed	selfish	dynamic	calm
guilty	angry	enthusiastic	centered
inadequate	annoyed	focused	adequate
sad	belligerent	happy	free
anxious	defiant	humor	integrity
cautious	furious	alive	alert

Creating an Inner Climate to "Catch Excellence"

In order to perform close to your potential, you must create an inner climate that allows you to perform easily. When I ran that non-stop after the car accident, I skied effortlessly. I had created an inner climate—albeit unknowingly—in which I was emotionally numb and therefore calm, focused, and relaxed. James Loehr, a sports psychologist and author of *Mental Toughness Training for Sports*, calls this the "Ideal Performance State," a condition of "physical energy, mental clarity, and emotional calm."

When understanding your inner climate as you compete, you must consider two factors: energy levels and emotional experiences. The energy level could be high, low, or anywhere in between. The emotional experience could be unpleasant, pleasant, or anywhere in between. When you draw it out, it looks like the grid below.

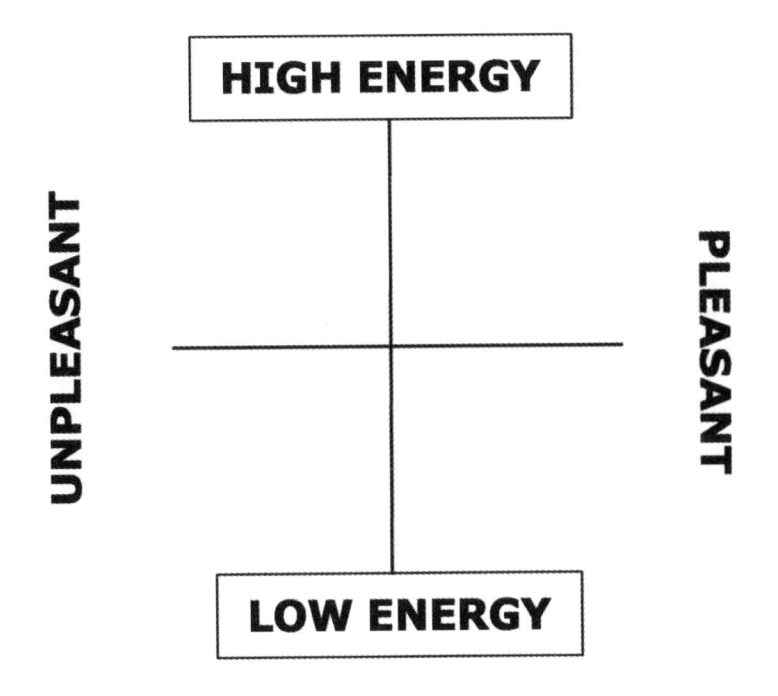

```
                    HIGH ENERGY
                         |
                         |
  UNPLEASANT  ———————————+———————————  PLEASANT
                         |
                         |
                    LOW ENERGY
```

The four quadrants represent different inner climates. An athlete who has low energy and an unpleasant experience may feel drained, burned out, depressed, hopeless, or psyched out. These emotions have little or no energy attached to them. Anyone who recognizes they are in this quadrant must understand that there is *no way* they will do well.

What can you do? You either decide that you need a break, and you give yourself some down time, *or* you accept the fact that this competition is more important. In that case, you adjust your attitude, acknowledge how you're feeling, and remind yourself that you *love* your sport and the competition. Reassure yourself that you *can* do this. Daydream about a competition where you felt great and loved every minute of it. In order to compete even moderately well, you must move out of this quadrant.

If you look at the lower right quadrant, again, there is low energy, but the experience is pleasant. The emotions here are more from tiredness or running out of gas. You're still excited about competing, but you just don't have energy. When you're competing from this space, you can only have limited success. You'll do better than the competitors in the low energy/unpleasant quadrant, but probably not any better than any other athletes.

In some sports, however, there are times when an athlete needs to float from the higher energy/pleasant quadrant to the low energy/pleasant quadrant. For instance, in games like field hockey, soccer, basketball, hockey, and baseball where the competition lasts for forty-five minutes or longer, an athlete cannot maintain that intensity for that long a period of time. Moving into the low energy/pleasant quadrant gives an athlete recovery time. However, when the ball or puck is in your space and you either need to defend or score, that low energy/pleasant quadrant just doesn't work!

Most athletes compete from the upper left quadrant, the high energy/unpleasant quadrant. Here, an athlete experiences nervousness, frustration, anxiety, fear, annoyance, jealousy, or anger. These feelings have a higher level of energy attached to them. Many athletes do well from this quadrant, and some even win major competitions. Again, I always think of John McEnroe, who had unbelievable success on the tennis circuit, but I've always wondered how he would have done if he had been able to lose his anger and completely enjoy his competitions. I believe that he would have been unstoppable!

HOW TO GAIN THE COMPETITIVE EDGE WORKSHEET

Many people question why anger is on the unpleasant side. Many competitors claim that they actually do better when they get angry. That was true for me, too. Anger does not, however, move you horizontally into the pleasant quadrant. It just moves you vertically and simply increases your energy level. You do better because you have more energy.

Competitors who have peak performances while in the zone or experience flow participate in their sport from this upper right-hand side—the high energy/pleasant quadrant. Here, the exertion is effortless because the athlete is motivated, focused, and calm; he loves what he's doing, he takes pride in himself and his effort, and he gains tremendous satisfaction in being part of the team. He feels excited, optimistic, confident, enthusiastic, and happy. Michael Jordan is an outstanding example of an athlete who was able to compete from this quadrant 90% of the time. He *loved* to play basketball!

On the next page, identify where the emotions fall that you circled from the previous exercise. Also, notice under what conditions you experienced those emotions. Is it when you are training? Competing? At home? Away? Singles? Doubles? Slalom? Downhill? Batting? Fielding?

The importance of this exercise is to understand which quadrant you fit into when you are performing and when the results matter to you, not just in competition but when you are trying to make a team or learning a new skill, for example. To do the best you can, you need to be in the upper right quadrant.

"The more focused I get, the more I can compete well under stress."
Dan O'Brien, 1996 Olympic Gold Medalist, Decathlon

Often an athlete can tell how he will do based on how he feels before the competition starts. When I work with ski racers, I like to ask them to consider how they felt before their run, when they were standing in the start. I ask them to think of a time when they were happy with how things went and then compare it to how they felt when things did not go well, and they were disappointed in their result. Often, the emotions they felt before they raced were high energy, pleasant emotions, while the emotions they felt when they were not happy with the result were low energy, unpleasant emotions.

How to Gain the Competitive Edge Worksheet

Evaluating the Inner Climate

Look over the feelings you circled when you completed the *Emotions* exercise. Which quadrant do they fit in? Is there a difference between when you practice and when you compete? Is there a difference in the location where the competition takes place (i.e., home field or away)? Is there a difference when you perform a certain skill (i.e., batting vs. fielding)? Or is there a difference when you compete in different events (i.e., slalom vs. giant slalom or singles vs. doubles)?

Once you've identified the quadrant and noticed the circumstances, there should be a correlation between the results and which quadrant most of those emotions fall into. Do you compete better than you train? Do you train better than you compete? Or are they just about even and there is not much difference between the two?

Are your results better at home or when you compete further from home? Do you do better in singles or doubles? Slalom or downhill? Offensively or defensively?

HIKE THE COURSE

HIGH ENERGY

UNPLEASANT	**PLEASANT**
Nervous Anxious Scared Tense Frustrated Angry Annoyed Jealous	Loving Motivated Optimistic Vigorous Peak Performance Calm "In the Zone" Joyful
Sick Burned-Out Depressed Bored Psyched-Out Hopeless	Sick Tired Out-of-Gas

LOW ENERGY

CHAPTER 13

Thoughts

I have a confession to make. After writing several of these chapters, I began to procrastinate on writing the rest of the book. I was proud of my work up to this point and I felt like I had done an extremely good job. I shared my work with friends, family, and other people whom I thought might be interested. I was confident that the feedback I would get would be good. And it was! The more I put it out, however, the more scared I became that I wouldn't be able to finish the remaining chapters as well as I had composed the first several. I actually set it aside for 12 years, but now I am determined to complete it!

One athlete with whom I've consulted about "gaining the competitive edge" was a figure skater who confided that she wasn't so afraid of mastering a particular jump. Instead, her greatest fear was that she would lose that skill after she conquered it. I know exactly how she feels.

As a coach, I often reassure an athlete that once they have performed a skill, they have proof that they are capable of completing that action. Since their nerves have created a path to their muscles once before, it can be repeated.

Yet, for me in writing this book, I began to let fear take over. I found it harder and harder to sit down and write. I finally had to sit back and reflect, reminding myself of my own coaching. Because I have created a mixture of personal stories, helpful information, quotes, checklists, and worksheets for athletes to complete, I have my model for completing the rest of the book. I know the layout and the fonts that I have already used. I just have to fill in the rest. I can break it down into small chunks and complete it step-by-step and chapter-by-chapter.

"Inch by inch, it's a cinch."
A. L. Williams, Author of All You Can Do is All You Can Do: But All You Can Do is Enough!

This example brings me to the current chapter where I would like to address how powerful our thoughts are. In the last chapter, I explained how emotions drive performance. I also described how emotions are connected to the brain and, unless there is an "emotional hijacking," the emotional mind is influenced by the thinking mind.

Napoleon Hill uses a poem in his book, *Think and Grow Rich*, to emphasize the power of thoughts:

If you think you are beaten, you are,
If you think you dare not, you don't.
If you like to win, but you think you can't,
It is almost certain you won't.

If you think you'll lose, you're lost,
For out in the world we find,
Success begins with a fellow's will—
It's all in the state of mind.

If you think you are outclassed, you are,
You've got to think high to rise,

*You've got to be sure of yourself before
You can ever win a prize.*

*Life's battles don't always go.
To the stronger or faster man,
But soon or late the man who wins.
Is the man who thinks he can!*

The Thinking Mind/Feeling Mind Connection

As I referred to in a previous section, the brain's emotional center is in the structures known as the amygdala, two small almond-shaped formations near the top of the brainstem. The amygdala enables one to feel emotions and to recognize those emotions in others. Meanwhile, the brain's thinking center is in the neocortex, which is made up of lots of sensory centers.

Usually, the emotional route follows this path: a situation occurs (i.e., an athlete gets tripped), and all of the information is sent to the brain via a structure called the thalamus that sends the messages to the neocortex (the thinking mind) and then on to the amygdala (the feeling mind). At that point, the athlete reacts emotionally and may feel angry or frustrated. As long as the natural alarm system is not activated and the emotions do not flood the amygdala and create an emotional hijacking, the athlete can maintain control of his behavior. He may realize that his opponent did not intentionally mean to trip him or that he simply missed the ball. The athlete could conclude that his opponent was not trying to hurt or humiliate him. Although he may still feel frustration, he does not move on to rage.

Emotions are not something that a person controls. Emotions happen to us since they are reactions from some event that has transpired. As the McGill University's website explains, "Emotions are something that happen to us much more than something we decide to make happen" (http://www.thebrain.mcgill.ca).

If emotions drive performance and an athlete has no control over choosing the emotions that are necessary to execute well, how does the athlete produce the emotions to create an inner climate to achieve excellence?

Managing Emotions Through Thoughts

In an earlier chapter, I explained how intense feelings override the thinking brain and result in an emotional hijacking. In this chapter, I will clarify how to access the emotions that create a positive inner climate by controlling thoughts.

I remember a time when I was high school. On the spur of the moment, I decided that I would try to scare my sister. We were returning home one evening and it was pitch black. We lived in the country and had no street lights or even an outside light. The parking spot for the car was about 30 yards from the porch. As we crossed the yard, I told her, "I think I hear a bear!"

I knew that I hadn't really heard anything, but the suggestion did work. She ran to the house and couldn't get in fast enough! Suddenly, as my thoughts changed from playing a prank on my sister to actually considering whether a bear might be in the yard, I also got scared. The likelihood of a bear being in our yard was highly improbable because there had never been a bear in our yard. The closest that they might be would be in the woods up in the hills behind our house. At that point, however, my thoughts were convincing me that there might actually be a creature lurking in the dark just outside my vision. I did not want to be mauled by a bear or anything else! In response, I also ran to the house in fear.

Why did I run in fright? Had I heard or seen anything to indicate that I might be in danger? No. My senses gave me no warning that something was about to harm me. I was afraid because I allowed my thoughts to create a situation in my mind that would have been dangerous, had it been true. I was afraid because I allowed myself to think a thought that was frightening.

We cannot control our emotions, but we can manage our thoughts. To create the emotions that we need to perform well, we must generate thoughts to produce those emotions. Remember that the emotions leading to a peak experience or competition that is within the zone are the emotions in the upper right quadrant—loving what you're doing, having fun, being excited and proud, feeling energetic and stimulated, feeling confident and enthusiastic, and enjoying your sport or team.

The thoughts that lead to these emotions and the upper-right quadrant are those that believe that you are capable, that you can do whatever is required of you, and that look forward to the challenge and the opportunity of competing.

"Self-discipline begins with the mastery of your thoughts. If you don't control what you think, you can't control what you do. Simply, self-discipline enables you to think first and act afterward."
Napoleon Hill, Author of Think and Grow Rich

The Thought Cycle

The thought cycle suggests that our ideas—the thoughts in our mind—produce emotions, which in turn affect how we behave. That behavior influences the results. Take a look at the figure below and the example that follows to illustrate the importance of the thought cycle.

The Thought Cycle

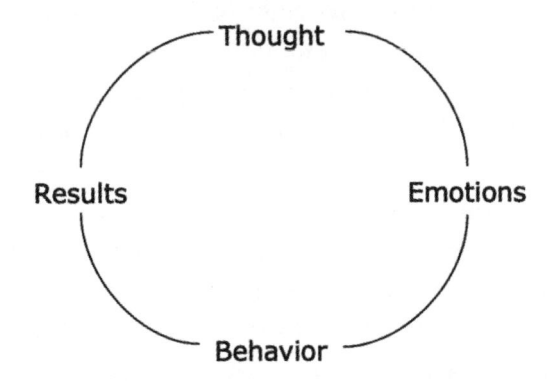

Thought → Emotions → Behavior → Results → (Thought)

Thoughts: One of the athletes I've worked with in ski racing admitted that, when he was at the start of the race, he looked at all of the racers ahead of him and thought, "They are so good! I'll never be able to ski as well as they can!" The more he contemplated, the more nervous he got. This went on until about twenty minutes before he started and he would be off in the woods, throwing up. His thoughts literally made him sick!

Emotions: Because he wanted to do well but doubted that he could ever be as good as the others, he became nervous, nauseous, scared, frustrated, and anxious.

Behavior: Every emotion elicits a specific body response. With all of those emotions pouring through his body when he got on the course, his muscles were tense, and his movements were jerky. Everything he did took effort, from breathing and flexing his muscles to powering his turns.

Results: When his muscles were tight and jerky, he could not ski well, so the results were less than satisfactory. He was not coming at all close to his potential achievement level.

His parents didn't know what to do to help him. When I met with him, we talked about his thoughts before the race and in the start. To manage his thoughts, we decided that doing his best was all he could ask of himself. Before the race and in the start, he changed his thoughts to "I'm just going to do the best I can!" and "This is so much fun! I love racing at Stratton!"

In the next few days, he raced in States at Stratton. He did extremely well and no longer got sick before his races. He was able to change his whole experience by managing his thoughts.

How to Gain the Competitive Edge Worksheet

The Thought Cycle

We cannot control our emotions. When something happens, we react to it emotionally. If someone says something encouraging, we feel good; if someone criticizes us, we get angry, sad, and upset; if we see something horrible, we feel shocked, disgusted, and sickened; and if we think scary thoughts, we experience fear.

Although we can't dictate our emotions, we can manage our thoughts. Our thoughts have tremendous impact on how we perform because our emotions are controlled by our thoughts.

As you picture your next competition, what *thought(s)* do you have as you wait to start? Then, record how that thought makes you feel (*emotions*). How do those emotions affect your *behavior*? What happens to the *results* because of that behavior?

The Thought Cycle

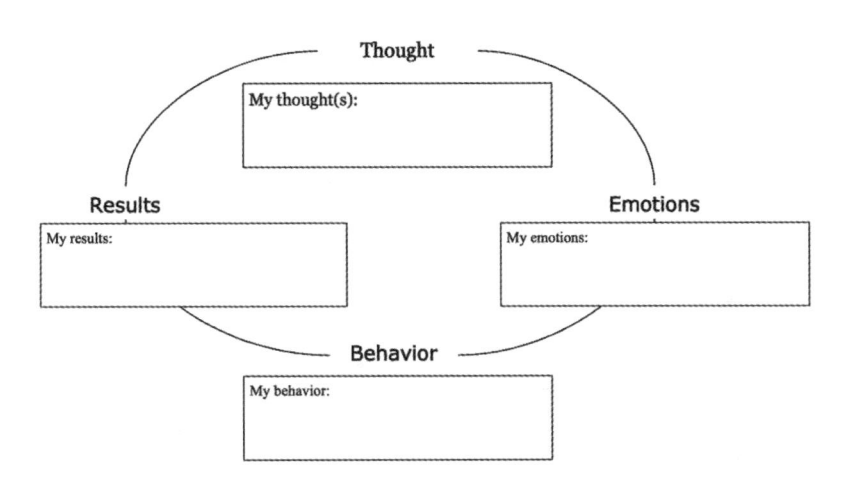

Thought
My thought(s):

Emotions
My emotions:

Behavior
My behavior:

Results
My results:

Pressure-Producing vs. Pressure-Reducing Thoughts

Some thoughts produce pressure, while other thoughts reduce pressure. The ideas that produce pressure are those that generate the unpleasant emotions—fear, anxiousness, nervousness, frustration, anger, annoyance, vengefulness, feeling overwhelmed, and the list goes on. These can also be referred to as "Fixed Mindset Thoughts," or the thoughts that judge how you are either performing or going to perform. They focus primarily on the results.

On the other hand, the ideas that reduce pressure are those that generate pleasant emotions—love, enjoyment, excitement, having fun, happiness, pride, enthusiasm, delight, feeling energetic, being stimulated, inspiration, facing a challenge, confidence, and more. These are the "Growth Mindset Thoughts," or the thoughts that fill you with optimism and a sense of opportunity. They shift the focus to the process.

Pressure-Producing Thoughts (Fixed Mindset Thoughts)

Thoughts that produce pressure are those where there is no freedom in how you perform–the shoulds, wants (or don't wants), and have-tos. "We should be confident because they're such a bad team!" "I want to win!" "I don't want to fall!" "I have to skate perfectly!"

Results-oriented thoughts tend to be pressure-producing. These are those that are concerned with:

- winning
- scoring
- beating a particular athlete
- not being beaten by a particular athlete
- finishing in the top category
- qualifying for a special team or competition
- striking out the batter or throwing a strike

Similarly, focusing on what you don't want to happen is also pressure-producing:

- not wanting to lose
- not wanting to fall, throw wildly, miss the goal or basket, etc.
- not wanting to fail at a particular skill.
- not wanting to disappoint the team, coach, parents, country, etc.

Then there are the "What if I don't succeed" scenarios:

- What if I lose? I'll never live it down!
- What if he hits a home run! We'll lose the game!

- What if I miss that jump?
- What if I get hurt?

When an athlete thinks, "I've got to . . ." then that thought also produces pressure:

- I've got to perform perfectly!
- I've got to out-run the opponent!
- I've got to set my personal best!
- I've got to strike this batter out!

Pressure-producing thoughts allow no freedom. There is no forgiveness and no slack. Pressure-producing thoughts expect results. Anything else is seen as failure. Pressure-producing thoughts bring up the wrong kind of emotions—the unpleasant emotions that create tension, stiffness, and an inability to perform easily and effortlessly.

Once an athlete recognizes that he is experiencing pressure-producing thoughts, he can change those thoughts to pressure-reducing and will generate the pleasant emotions in the upper right quadrant that lead to his ability to perform easily and effortlessly.

Pressure-Reducing Thoughts (Growth Mindset Thoughts):

Thoughts that reduce pressure are those in which there is freedom in how you perform—the coulds, wills, and mays. Rather than thinking, "We should be confident because they're such a bad team!" you can think, "We could do well because they're an inexperienced team." Rather than saying, "I don't want to fall!" or "I have to skate perfectly!" consider changing it to, "I will just do my best!"

Whenever I stood in the start, I told myself, "I'm just going to do the best that I can!" That gave me the freedom to do what I could do on that particular day and under those circumstances. My best could have been placing first, last, or anywhere in between, but as long as that was my best, I would have to accept it. I might not be happy or satisfied with the results, but if that was truly my best, I couldn't have done anything more.

At the Olympics, I reduced the pressure by managing my thoughts. I fought to stay calm. I reminded myself, "I can only do my best." I built up my confidence by thinking, "If the French girls can win, I can, too!" I even prepared myself for defeat by thinking, "Even if I don't win, I've won the first run and not very many people have done that! So, no matter what, I can always be proud of what I've accomplished."

That doesn't mean that an athlete should settle for mediocrity. It just means that when chasing excellence, an athlete's results will sometimes go her way and sometimes they will not.

The two most helpful pressure-reducing thoughts that I have found are "I'm just going to do the best I can!" and "This is so much fun! I LOVE _____!" (Fill in the blank to include playing soccer, baseball, field hockey, and ski racing to hitting against this pitcher, scoring goals, dodging, tackling, and more).

"Although I wanted my players to work to win, I tried to convince them they had always won when they had done their best."
John Wooden, Former UCLA Basketball Coach and Teacher

On the following page, identify any pressure-producing or

fixed mindset thoughts that you may have. Are there others that are not on the list? Record those in the space provided.

Now look at the pressure-reducing and growth mindset thoughts. What thoughts would work for you? What other thoughts could help you reduce the pressure? Write those down as well.

Until you've developed the habit of thinking pressure-reducing thoughts, write down the ideas that are most helpful on index cards and carry them with you. Just before you compete, refresh your memory with one or two. You will be amazed at the change in your inner climate and your ability to perform.

Some athletes with whom I've worked even carry their index card with them to help them prepare for the start of their competitive activity. Just before they get in the starting gate, they take a look at their prompts and read these words aloud:

- I'm just going to do the best I can!
- I **can** do this!
- This is so much fun! I **love** _____ (fill in the blank)!

The last thing that I always recommend doing is to smile. When you smile, it releases some of the stress and reinforces each of the above points.

How To Gain The Olympic Edge Worksheet

Thoughts

Pressure-Producing Thoughts/Fixed Mindset Thoughts

1. What if I don't do well!
2. What if I blow it now!
3. What if I make the wrong decision—I'll get fired!
4. The coach is counting on me—if I make a mistake, I'll get benched!
5. The pressure is too much!
6. I'll never live it down if I lose!
7. I've got to do well—my parents are watching!
8. I've got to beat _____!
9. I've got to finish in the top or I won't qualify for _____.

My pressure-producing thoughts:

1.
2.
3.

Pressure-Reducing Thoughts/Growth Mindset Thoughts

1. I'm just going to do the best I can.
2. I'm going to focus on doing my job the best I know how.

HOW TO GAIN THE OLYMPIC EDGE WORKSHEET

3. This is so much fun!
4. Pressure is something I put on myself.
5. Even if I'm not the greatest today, it won't be the end of the world.
6. Winning and losing is for the fans; I simply perform.
7. I love tough situations; the tougher the situation, the better I perform.
8. I'm going to be okay—no matter what.
9. I **LOVE** _____ (ski racing, baseball, tennis, competing against etc.)

My pressure-reducing thoughts:

1.
2.
3.

(Information from James Loehr's book, Mental Toughness Training for Sports.*)*

CHAPTER 14

Affirmations

You may have reached the point where you believe you want to be successful, where you believe you deserve to be successful, and where you believe you can be successful, but that belief is not enough until you take action—until you accept it at a deep emotional level. To accept it at this level, you must identify and confront the emotional obstacles. This is where the subconscious comes in to play.

You can have only one primary belief, feeling, or idea. If you have two, the subconscious will accept only the dominant one. Another interesting characteristic about the subconscious is that it cannot distinguish between what is real and what is imagined. If you present the subconscious with images that seem vivid and real, it will accept them as real. So, imagining that you are a talented, skillful, and successful person—whether that means you fill the role of an athlete, coach, parent, teacher, or student—means that you will convince your brain, which then convinces your body, which then results in a person (*you!*) who walks, talks, breathes, looks, and acts like a successful _____ (fill the blank with your favorite role).

The Rule of the Three P's

One means to convince your mind that you are talented, skillful, and successful is to use affirmations. An affirmation is a statement that describes how you would like to be. In order for an affirmation to appear real, it must follow the rules of the three **P's.** The affirmation must be stated.

1. **Positively**, since the subconscious does not acknowledge negatives;
2. In the **first person** ("I" for an individual or "we" for a group or team); and
3. In the **present tense,** as if it is actually happening right now.

An affirmation is a tool that can be used in one of two ways—either to discover what your dominant, subconscious beliefs are, or to change the way that you currently operate.

When I was a ski racer in the '60s and '70s, I had never heard of or been taught about affirmations before. In spite of that, because I answered the same question over and over, I actually did use an affirmation. When people asked me how I thought I would do at the Olympics, my response was always the same: "I don't know if I will win at the Olympics, but what I do know is that I am capable of winning!" In the deepest part of my soul, I was confident. There was no question in my mind! I knew I was as good as anyone else in that race. The message to my subconscious mind was, "Yes, of course, you can do it!" The night before the Olympic slalom, the thought occurred to me that "Someone has to win! So, why not me?"

When I first heard of affirmations many years later, I was reading an autobiography of Dan Jansen, who was a dominant speed skater in the '80s and '90s. He wrote a book called *Full Circle*, which chronicled his athletic career spanning four Olympics, from Sarajevo in 1984 to Lillehammer in 1994. In his first Olympics, Dan was young, only 16 years old, which was considered up-and-coming. By his second

Olympics in Calgary in 1988, he was expected to win gold in the 500-meter race.

Unfortunately, he received news the morning before his race that his sister, Jane, with whom he was extremely close, had died of leukemia. She had been sick for a long time, and he already knew that she was dying, but he felt torn because she had died before his race. He felt guilty that he was in Calgary and not at home with her, although he did not realize that he was facing such a conflict in that moment. Even though he had dominated the 500-meter races leading up to the Olympics, at those games, he fell.

When Dan competed at the next Olympics in Albertville in 1992, he once again was the dominant 500-meter speed skater and was expected to win the gold medal. But, once again, he failed to win any medals. Between his third Olympics in Albertville and his fourth Olympics in Lillehammer, his coach recommended that he take some time to receive counseling. Through therapy, Dan realized that he was experiencing a sense of guilt at the Olympics, which went all the way back to when Jane first passed away. He came to realize that he had not forgiven himself for choosing the Olympics over being with his beloved sister as she was dying. (In all fairness to Dan, I often wonder if it was his sister's way to be with him as he competed in Calgary!)

At that point, Dan knew that Lillehammer would be his last Olympics. Although he raced in the 1000 meters as well as the 500 meters, his best event was the 500 meters. As usual, leading up to the Olympics, he dominated that event. This time, one important thing had changed. When Dan first went to counseling, the therapist suggested that he begin using several different affirmations. One affirmation addressed the issue of his ability to excel in the 1000 meters. Dan originally believed that if he was a good 500-meter speed skater, he could not be as good in the 1000 meters because they were just too different.

However, Dan began practicing an affirmation that he loved racing the 1000 meters. He said that it made him feel like an elementary school kid as he wrote the affirmation down: "I love racing the 1000 meters!" He put that message on index cards and then posted those cards everywhere—in the drawer where he kept his razor, in the car, in his bedroom, with his notebooks where he recorded his workouts, anywhere and everywhere that he would regularly see them.

What happens with written affirmations is that, even when you are not consciously aware of reading those notes, your brain receives that message. The subconscious mind then tries to make whatever the message says come true. That season, after bombarding his brain with the message that he loved racing the 1000 meters, Dan actually did well in that event! So, leading up to the speed skating events in Lillehammer, Dan was favored to win the 500 meters and also do well in the 1000 meters.

When the day of the Olympics in Lillehammer finally arrived, the 500-meter race was scheduled just before the 1000-meter race. Once again, Dan did not win the 500 meters. He began to feel very frustrated that he would never accomplish his goal of winning an Olympic gold medal, but then his coach gave him an excellent idea, suggesting that the greatest ending to his story would be that he actually would win gold—not in the 500 meters but in the 1000 meters. And that is exactly what Dan did!

Preparation for Exercises on Affirmations

Go back to the page where you recorded your present beliefs. What were your weaknesses? Choose one of the beliefs and write an affirmation so that it changes the weakness into a strength. Write it in the present tense.

Example: If you feel like you can never make a foul shot when you play basketball, write an affirmation that states just the opposite. "I always make foul shots when I play basketball!" You can even add emotion to it to make it more powerful. "I LOVE taking foul shots!"

Affirmations

Exercise 1: The Blurts—To Discover My Dominant, Subconscious Beliefs

On a blank, lined page, write an affirmation. For instance, you might write: "I am a talented and skillful (athlete, coach, parent, teacher, student, person . . .)." Leave three blank lines after the affirmation and write it again on the fifth line. Repeat until the page is filled with the affirmation with three blank lines in between each phrase.

The exercise might look something like this:

> I am a talented and skillful ski racer!
> _____
> _____
>
> I am a talented and skillful ski racer!
> _____
> _____
>
> I am a talented and skillful ski racer!
> _____
> _____
>
> I am a talented and skillful ski racer!

Now, go back and read your affirmation out loud. Once you have read the statement, listen to the chatter that goes on in your head. These are called "blurts," which are the subconscious mind's way to let you know how you truly feel. Write down the blurts after reading the first line. Then read the affirmation again on the fifth line and write down the blurts you "hear" on the blank lines. Continue throughout the page. When you reach the bottom, you may stop or go back and begin at the top again. Repeat, until you run out of blurts.

The blurts might sound something like this:

> I am a talented and skillful ski racer!
> **What??? Who are you trying to kid?**
>
> _____
>
> I am a talented and skillful ski racer!
> **Everybody is better than me!**
>
> _____
>
> I am a talented and skillful ski racer!
> **I can't even beat _____ (fill in the blank)!**
>
> _____
>
> I am a talented and skillful ski racer!

This exercise accomplishes two things. First, it lets you know what your subconscious mind truly feels or believes. Secondly, every time you write a blurt down on paper, it releases some of the power that it had over you. In other words, that dominant belief becomes less powerful, and that belief becomes easier to change. (Warning: If your blurts were reinforcing the negative belief, then that belief actually becomes stronger!)

Exercise 2: Affirmation Declarations—To Change My Reality and My Subconscious Beliefs

When you write an affirmation, remember to follow the rule of the three **P's**. Each one must be:

1. From the point of view of the first **P**erson,
2. Stated **P**ositively, and
3. Stated in the **P**resent tense.

Affirmations are powerful tools to change one belief that is presently true for you, but undesired, into a belief that will become true for you, which is desired. For instance, if you always strike out when you get up to bat, you might have a belief that goes something like this: "I'm the worst batter on the team! I always strike out! I hate batting!"

With those kinds of beliefs, your subconscious mind is working hard to make sure that those beliefs are accurate. As a result, your subconscious mind will do its best to help you strike out, make sure you're the worst batter on the team, and reinforce that you hate batting. In order to become a better batter, then, you need to first change the beliefs in your subconscious mind. You do that by stating what you *want* to be true *as if it already were true!*

Some athletes feel like this is lying to your subconscious mind. It is, in a sense, but only because you already believe what is in your subconscious mind. **Your beliefs are true only because you believe them to be true!** Your coach may recognize your potential and not agree with the conclusions that you have come up with. So, if you really want to change your beliefs, you must state what you want to be true as if it already is.

In the case of the baseball player, he could make the following affirmations to change his subconscious beliefs to become a better batter:

1. "I LOVE batting!"
2. "I always get a hit against this pitcher!"
3. "I am one of the best batters on the team!"

Take some time to list the beliefs that are true for you at this moment but are undesired.

1. _____
2. _____
3. _____

Now, rewrite each of those beliefs into a positive statement that you wish were true. Remember to write each one in the present tense as if it already were true for you.

1. _____
2. _____
3. _____

Tips for Affirmations

1. You may have more than three beliefs that you would like to change, but it is better to concentrate on no more than three at a time. When you first begin, choose the undesired beliefs that are the most important to change. Once you feel that you have changed your belief in one area, you can move on to another.
2. After you have written down your beliefs, make sure to review them often. I suggest using index cards, just like

Dan Jansen did. Write each affirmation on an index card with one affirmation per card. Use about ten index cards per affirmation and then put them in strategic places where you will regularly see them.

The most effective use of affirmations that I have ever seen were with two sisters who plastered their whole house with affirmations. When I walked into their house, everywhere I turned, there was an affirmation! They had them on the bathroom mirror, on the door jambs, on the lamp shades, on the refrigerator, on the bureau, on the headboard, on other furniture, and even in notebooks. You could not walk through that house without being bombarded with an affirmation!

The amazing thing to me was that they changed their beliefs in about two weeks! Their subconscious minds were receiving their affirmations hundreds of times a day. With that much repetition, they were able to change **undesired beliefs** into **desired beliefs** within just a couple weeks of starting the process.

1. I also suggest that you carry your affirmations with you, so you are constantly reminded of them. Use your imagination in figuring out where to put them. When my son was dreaming of racing in the big leagues, I noticed that he had put tape on his skis with a message to remind him of what he wanted to work on. I've long forgotten what the message was, but it was a simple one- or two-word phrase that helped him focus and send the message to his subconscious mind.

CHAPTER 15

Mental Rehearsal

Another tool to create the results that you want is mental rehearsal. The best thing about accessing your mind is that you can practice anywhere and at any time. Sometimes, athletes are not able to physically train, but they still have a desire to improve. Athletes can be sidelined because of injury, sickness, the "off-season," or simply because they do not have the financial ability to support their efforts. In all of these cases, improvement is not out of reach!

Athletes generally train before or after a competition, but once the competition is under way, they do not have the chance to physically practice. However, they can rehearse anytime as much as they want through mental exercise. For example, before a basketball player takes a foul shot, she can visualize the ball leaving her hands, arcing through the air, and swishing through the basket. A golfer can imagine the ball landing exactly where he wants it to go. A tennis player can see the ball as she serves it into her opponent's court. A ski racer can practice his run exactly as he wishes, many times before he even hits the slopes for his race.

When I first made the U.S. Ski Team, our coach encouraged us to read *Psycho-Cybernetics* by Maxwell Maltz. In that book, I learned how powerful the mind can be in developing skill within your sport. One thing that especially stood out to me was how Maltz described a basketball study in which the researcher wanted to find out if athletes could improve their free throws simply by using their minds.

The Basketball Study

In this study, the athletes were divided randomly into three groups. The first group was asked to practice free throws for an hour every day for a whole month, the second group was asked to visualize throwing free throws, and the third group did neither. At the end of the month, the athletes in the first group had improved by 24%, the athletes in the second group had improved by 23% without even having touched a basketball, and the athletes in the third group had not improved at all.

Is it possible for you to improve without actually practicing your sport? Absolutely! When we regularly use mental techniques—which may also be known as using visualization, mental imagery, or mental rehearsal—then we can see our skills being improved, just like the basketball players did in the study.

"All successful people use it consciously or unconsciously, attracting the success they want into their life, by visualizing their goals as already accomplished."
Remez Sasson, Author and Motivational Speaker

One important component of mental rehearsal is visualization. Visualization works because the subconscious mind cannot tell the difference between what is real and what is imagined. In fact, the subconscious mind treats the thoughts and images that are created in our minds as if they were real. Athletes can use this to their advantage and improve their skills either by physically practicing a movement or by simply **imagining** the movement!

When I was a young ski racer, I knew that in order to get better I would have to get on the snow, listen to my coach (my dad), and try to put into practice what he told me. Sometimes, I tried to improve by working on my turns when I was free-skiing and, other times, I tried to improve by running gates. Either way, my mental thought was always that the actual training on snow was the only thing that would lead to my improvement.

My dad had a revelation one day when he was coaching us, however, and he noticed that his ski racers always seemed to drop a significant amount of time during training after we reached our third or fourth run. He wondered why that was happening consistently to all of us.

Then it suddenly dawned on him. "It's because they know the course!"

Then my dad began to think about how we could capitalize on his discovery. We knew that we could not take a couple of runs over a course on race day to learn it or we would be disqualified, so how could a racer achieve the same advantage? Dad felt that if we memorized the course, we essentially could take as many runs as we wanted without actually running it.

This was my first introduction to using my mind as a way to train.

Techniques

There are three techniques to draw upon for these mental practice sessions:

1. Visualization
2. Observation
3. Self-talk

Visualization: Even as a ten-year-old, Dad had used this technique. He told the story that when he was learning how to pitch, he would take a baseball to bed with him. Before he fell asleep, he would practice holding the ball with different grips for different pitches. By the time he was in high school, he had perfected his pitches. He went on to pitch in college and in the minor leagues before retiring from baseball.

To use another example of a baseball pitcher, Tug McGraw used visualization years before he became a professional player. As a child, Tug played catch in his backyard with his dad. They always ended the session with him imagining that he was in the ninth inning of the World Series with bases loaded and two outs. He was pitching and always managed to strike the next batter out. When it actually came to pass years later, Tug had practiced that scene so many times that it was no big deal. He *knew* that he would get the batter out because he had done it over and over as a kid.

There are five important steps to visualization:

1. Be very clear with what you want to accomplish. Ask yourself the following questions:
   - Is this something that I truly want to achieve?
   - Will this be good for me?
   - How do I execute these skills or achieve this result?
2. Find a place where you can imagine the circumstances without being disturbed.
   - For example, when I was ski racing, I memorized every single course that I raced when I was on the hill. There were other competitors all around me, but I just closed my eyes and imagined myself running the course in solitude.
   - Other times, I visualized ski racing after I had gone to bed. I would lie there before I went to sleep and go through every turn and gate in my mind.

3. Think about the things that could go wrong.
   - What do you worry about? By identifying those things, you can come up with a plan about what you can do instead.
   - For instance, if you have the habit of skiing out after you make a mistake, you can make a commitment to yourself before you leave the start: *I will always try to make the next gate, no matter how much trouble I get into!*
4. Visualize exactly what you want to accomplish.
   - Make the experience as real as possible by using all five of your senses—sight, touch, sound, taste, and smell.
   - Visualize every time before you execute the skills, regardless of whether you are competing or simply training.
   - For example, I was often scared to run downhill. To improve my skills and face my fears, I would *mentally rehearse* running the downhill before I fell asleep at night. I would take 5 to 10 runs each night. Because of that, I was able to finish 14th twice in World Cup downhills!
   - Relax and breathe deeply.
5. Stay positive: Positive thoughts, positive feelings, positive words!
   - When negative thoughts come into your head, replace them with positive thoughts.

Observation: Observation means that you watch videos of the athletes in your sport who execute the skills easily, as well as videos of yourself. Steve Lathrop was one of the participants on the U.S. Ski Team when I was on the team during the '70s. He told me that when he was at Holderness, he started watching lots and lots of films every day after classes that showed the best ski racers in the world. He believes that his skills improved because of that. From there, Steve was able to make the U.S. Ski Team and compete at the World Championships in Val Gardena, Italy.

When practicing observation, the steps are similar to those for visualization:

1. Focus on what you want to improve.
3. Find a time and place where you won't be disturbed.
4. Stay positive! Always be looking out for the things that you are doing well, as well as for the things that you want to improve.

Self-talk: Affirmations are just one example of self-talk. They work because of the way that the brain works. The sub-conscious mind cannot tell the difference between what is real and what is imagined. When you talk to yourself, your mind will try to make it happen, regardless of whatever you are telling it.

For example, if you tell yourself, "I never will be as good as _____!" (fill in the blank with your greatest competitor), then your mind will try to make sure that you will never be as good as them. Go back and review Chapter 14 for help on developing your affirmations in order to overturn such negative thoughts.

To use a personal example, when I first made the U.S. Ski Team, I was in awe of the Europeans and especially admired the French girls. I put them on a pedestal and did not believe that I could ski as well as they could.

Eventually, however, I began to tell myself, "If the French girls can win, I can, too!" By the time I got to the Olympics, I believed in the deepest part of my soul that I could ski with the best of them. That belief led to my ability to win the slalom!

Using Mental Rehearsal When Training

When you actually get to the point of training, you can combine all three techniques to get the most out of your session.

1. Start with a video session and focus on watching athletes performing the specific skill that you want to master.
2. Listen to your coach's advice and write it down. One or two simple sentences is all that you need.
3. When you go to bed at night, take a few minutes to visualize yourself performing the skill.
4. The next day, remind yourself what it is you are working on. Jot it down on an index card or write a word about it and then tape the card where you will see it. One athlete told me that he even wrote something on the back of his hand! Throughout the training session, picture the movement again.
5. When you are starting to execute the skill, focus again on what you are trying to master.
6. Repeat the process each day!

As you add mental rehearsal to your routine, you can make great strides by considering the following questions: What would I like to accomplish as an athlete? Is there a dream that I would like to achieve someday? Is there a specific skill that I would like to master?

It is time to write down your answers!

1. The dream I would like to achieve is
2. _____
3. _____

4. _____
5. A skill I would like to master is
6. _____
7. _____
8. _____

Commit to visualizing for ten minutes when you first wake up. Do it again for ten minutes before you fall asleep. Then visualize executing this skill each and every time you do it.

Mental rehearsal can lead to a perfect practice, which does not often happen with physical practice. Perfect practice is clearly superior to repeated poor performance during practice. Experiencing success increases confidence, even if that experience is imagined!

EPILOGUE

Our Passion

As I have reflected over the years on the Cochran Way that was started by my dad and formulated my own method for coaching athletes, I really am very happy with what we have been able to contribute to the world of sports. At first, it was incredibly amazing to me to realize that my whole family was making history with skiing in America, since it was simply something that we loved to do together every winter with our family and broader community.

Once I recognized the fact that we really were that good and our family was able to accomplish so much in our own racing on the U.S. Ski Team, I saw it as a great opportunity to give back. I wanted to pass on my knowledge to others who hoped to follow in our family's footsteps. I believe that with the coaching that I received from my father and other instructors, the material that I have gathered from different sources over the years, and my own experience being on the slopes, I am passing on a tremendous legacy to new people who are rising up in the ranks as today's athletes.

For "us Cochrans," it has always been about community. Growing up in small towns and different rural areas, we always knew the importance of having great people around us. We were part of a team and encouraged by a **winning team culture**. We were urged to compete in races against the best individuals available. We could learn from them and as we got better, they could learn from us. With this philosophy, the bar just gets higher and higher. Competition continually improves.

The World Cup races I competed in when I first travelled to Europe were a slalom and giant slalom in Oberstaufen, Germany. An American, Kiki Cutter, won the giant slalom. Our coach, Chuck Ferries, told us, "When one of us wins, we all win!" That is a "winning team culture."

By contrast, it has been disappointing for me to see some athletes and programs who do not have this team mindset at all. For the past couple of decades, some national teams in alpine racing, including the United States, have developed a model where a person who excels today tends to have their own team, their own coaches, and their own PT regimen, but they avoid sharing "their secret" with the greater team. The focus is to produce a winner, even if it's only one individual who excels. This is a **winning culture** or "win at all costs." There may be a team, but the standout individual is treated separately.

At that point, the rest of the sports community might be left wondering, "How does he prepare? Why was she so good? What is his technique?" and similar questions. In that kind of scenario, it does not appear that this athlete is the type of person who is willing to give back and make sure that the younger people rising up in the ranks are able to develop to their own full potential.

Going back to the lessons that Dad always taught us, he emphasized two specific lessons why we always need to be competing against the best skiers around us. One, it provides us with an accurate gauge to know where we are, whether we are at the top and, if not, then it helps us to know how to get there. Two, when we're competing with the absolute best, we are able to pick up tips and tricks from them to improve our own abilities, and they usually are things that we normally would not learn otherwise.

I learned those lessons on a very personal level when I was watching tennis on the TV channel for U.S. Open. After watching the game, I went right outside for my own game and immediately noticed that my play had greatly improved. I was not even aware of what it was that changed, but I had picked up things by simply watching athletes who were fantastic at their sport.

At the same time, I also realize that the team spirit also goes both ways. Perhaps there is a top athlete in any particular kind of sport who recognizes that they have the opportunity to be that kind of role model for the rest of the team. If they are willing to have others learn from them, but the team does not treat them with that same goal in mind, then it will not achieve the same effect.

That's not to say that an exceptional athlete doesn't have her needs met. She needs to train; she needs to be coached; she needs whatever to be able to perform to the best of her ability. But what I question is, does she need to be encapsulated and treated as if she is the only one on the team? I believe that philosophy is not healthy for the individual nor the team.

In my own experience dealing with the U.S. Ski Team, I unfortunately noticed that the emphasis over the last twenty years was support and raise up one individual who stands out from the rest of the team. The U.S. has had exceptional athletes with Bode Miller, Ted Ligety, Lindsey Vonn, and of course, Mikaela Shiffrin, and has embraced that kind of attitude. That approach, however, does not give back to the community nor provide the opportunity for a team to learn and push each other to higher and higher levels.

A team that has been successful in alpine skiing over the years and has supported a team approach, has been the Norwegians. As national teams take a look at their methodology, I do believe some countries, including the U.S., have begun to swing back to a more encompassing way of thinking.

Mikaela Shiffrin may be partially responsible for part of this shift. When she first broke on to the World Cup, it was evident she was talented. No one has been surprised that she is and has been a phenom. The U.S. Ski Team provided her with her own coaches, physical therapists, technicians, training times, and whatever else she needed on her "team." She was held above the rest of the women on the U.S. Ski Team and was not encouraged to integrate with them. Her U.S. Ski Team teammates did not know her, and she did not know them. The USST did not want the rest of the world to learn any of her "secrets," even the younger athletes coming up in the U.S.

But the pendulum is swinging back. She has been dating a Norwegian, Aleksander Aamodt Kilde, who has grown up under the Norwegian **winning team culture.** Has that had any impact on the development of the talent in the U.S.? I don't know, but Mikaela invited all members of the women's alpine team to a special weekend in Denver in the summer of 2023. They stayed in a hotel, had a special concert with Noah Kahan, went to the Taylor Swift concert, had a pickle ball tournament, and just hung out. Mikaela has the opportunity to become a leader on the U.S. women's alpine team to provide valuable skills to those around her, if she chooses.

Regardless of what others do, however, I continue to look forward. I am proud of how we have developed, and I have high hopes for how Cochran's will continue to grow under the ever-expanding family outfit. Our passion will always be about doing our very best, knowing that is enough, and passing on that same message to the whole community that surrounds us. As I face every new day with the attitude of working on my own mindset, I am excited to see many other athletes join our team and gain their own competitive edge that they need to reach their true potential!

Acknowledgments

I would like to acknowledge my family. Mom, Ginny, and Dad, Mickey, you taught me to dream and believe that with hard work and attention to detail, anything was possible.

To my siblings, Marilyn, Bobby, and Lindy, I can't imagine having better playmates and teammates with whom to grow up. You have led the way, encouraged me, supported me, inspired me, and provided a shoulder for me to cry on when times were tough.

To my children, Caitlin and Ryan and my grandchildren, you amaze me. I am so proud to be your mom and Ma'ama. To my nieces and nephews and great-nieces and great-nephews, aunts and uncles (including those who have passed), and cousins, family is everything. My life is filled with joy with all of you in it. And to my friends, you too are part of my family and have made my life richer.

I am forever grateful for my angel reader, Kourtney Levens for introducing me to my friend, Patti Fors, and my publisher, Muse Literary. Patti, I cannot imagine finishing this book without your guidance and inspiration. You made this project easy!

I love you all!
BA Cochran

About the Author

Barbara Ann Cochran is an Olympic gold medalist and a sought-after performance coach who works one on one with selected athletes training them to use their minds to achieve results of which they've only dreamed.

She is a member of the Cochran family from Richmond, Vermont, famously known as the "First Family of Skiing." Nine family members have competed in World Championships; six have also competed in the Olympics. Barbara Ann's son Ryan was the only alpine skier to medal at the 2022 Beijing Olympics. Clearly there is a method there that works!

Unlike textbook-trained sports psychologists, Barbara Ann has lived the dream, giving her unrivaled experience and a unique understanding of athletes' challenges. With 21 years of teaching experience and the proven success of "the Cochran Way," nothing makes Barbara Ann smile more than helping athletes, in any sport, gain the competitive edge.

She knows what it takes and feels like to be the best in the world.